Photo by Carol Savo

YOU CAN SEE DOLLY
IN PERSON ON DOLLY'S
PARLOR CAR TOUR ON THE
WHITE PASS & YUKON ROUTE RR
SKAGWAY, ALASKA

MEET DOLLY!

Madam Dolly & Dewey the Donkey from Liarsville

Photo by Renate Mulvihill

Photo by Stacy Eaton

CINDY LOU GODBEY

****

"HOOTS & TOOTS
ON
DOLLY'S
PARLOR CAR"

TRUE TALES OF AN ALASKAN ADVENTURESS

Photo by Carol Savo

Fun on Dolly's Parlor Car   Photo by Carol Savo

Balloons Over Alaska - page 19
Photo by Hugh McLellan

Dolly & Polar Bears - page 87
Photo by Cindy Shults

Printed and bound in the United States of America
First printing • ISBN 1-930043-77-5
Copyright © 2009 Cindy Godbey

Published by Scott Company Publishing
P.O. Box 9707 • Kalispell, MT 59904
Toll Free: 1-800-628-0212 • Fax: 1-406-756-0098

Please Contact for Book Order Information

To purchase Hoots & Toots
• See Dolly on Dolly's Parlor Car
• Local Skagway Businesses
• When you leave Skagway:
  Call 1-800-628-0212

TABLE OF CONTENTS

DEDICATION

*Madam Dolly & Donjek, a MacKenzie River Husky
at the Gold Rush Trail Camp in Liarsville, outside of Skagway.*

This book is dedicated to Will, my wonderful husband, who has always loved me, no matter what; to my sister Diane who saved me from going to an orphanage and for being my saving grace; to my brother Bill who gives me strength and support, and to Cara my niece, for always being a blessing to me. Thank you to Lorna and Heather, who helped make this book happen and to all my family and friends who gave me love, guidance and support through all my life's journeys. A big thank you to Jean Worley for always being there for me, to Jan Wrentmore who owns the Red Onion Saloon, for believing in me and discovering me at Moe's Frontier Bar, to Alina with NCL for getting me on Dolly's Parlor Car, and to everyone in Skagway for your friendship over the years and for providing the opportunity for Dawson Dolly to come to life. The wonderful times I have experienced with you all have given me the beautiful memories shared in this book! Thanks to Richard Thornhill for believing in me and encouraging me to write this book.

Most of all, I want to thank my Lord and Savior, Jesus Christ, for giving me a second chance in life. May God bless you all one hundred-fold.

Love, Dolly

TABLE OF CONTENTS

LIVING IN A JUNKYARD AND PLAYING WITH THE STARS

Before I became an Alaskan woman, I was a California girl. I spent eleven years in the sunshine state and lived all over the place. San Francisco, San Jose, Santa Cruz, Redwood Estates, Uvas Canyon, Gold Run…. Gold Run is just north of Sacramento. Population: 25. Town consisted of a bar and a post office. And my little cabin behind the bar, where I used to hold wild parties. The population would go up a bit, then everyone would stagger off home with a hangover and we'd be back down to 25. Lots of interesting places and crazy people. I guess I spent longer than I realized gathering experience for living in the north.

Living in a junkyard in San Jose was a real trip. I guess in a way it sort of prepared me for being the wife of a gold miner who feels he needs to save every nut and bolt from every piece of equipment he has ever owned, whether it still runs or not. It's like living on the set of "Sanford & Son."

I was living with Michael, owner of a towing company and auto body shop. He was also moonlighting as a repo-man. Taking away cars for missed payments tends to make people a bit cranky, so it was kind of a dangerous job. We actually lived behind locked gates in a towing yard full of cars. New cars, old cars, vintage cars, junked cars, we had 'em all. There was a warehouse/workshop in the front, and tucked behind it in an alley, amidst all the cars, was a 22 foot trailer. Home, sweet home. I called it "Tin City Motor Park."

We lived in the junkyard for a year. Then we had the chance to move out of town, so we packed up and headed to Uvas Canyon. We had 30 acres out there, called "Valentine Acres". Prior to our arrival, it was a nudist colony. They moved out, we moved in. It had a great many advantages over living in a junkyard. We would trap crawdads in the creek for our supper, and I raised peacocks, pheasants, chickens and goats. The only small drawback was the hour drive to and from work everyday.

At the time I was working in downtown San Jose, at a fancy hotel called "LeBaron Hotel". A lot of memories from that place. Like the time I was interviewed for the 25th Anniversary issue of Playboy magazine. I never did win, but it was sure flattering to be asked by the head bunny to come down and have my pictures taken.

I worked at the hotel for eight years. I loved it. I met a lot of interesting people. I worked on the top floor. It was a fancy place, called The Terrace. The Mafia boys came there a lot when they were on trial. I used to tell them mafia jokes and they would laugh. The Bonanos were great guys, but I was sure glad I wasn't one of their girlfriends.

I remember when the football teams were on strike and the owners of the teams came to the hotel to have a meeting. It lasted two weeks. I met the owner of the Miami Dolphins. He was a great guy. His name was Joe, but for the life of me, I can't remember his last name. He was an older gentleman, happily married with eleven kids. Quite a stud! He really took a liking to me, but more as a friend or a daughter. He invited me to his home in Montana and in Florida, he always told me he wanted to fix me up with one of the boys from the team. He gave me all his contact numbers and extended the invitation often, but I never did make it. I wonder where my life would have gone if I had taken that path? Maybe married to a football player and dripping in diamonds? But, the Lord had other plans for me.

Lots of famous people crossed my path when I worked there. One day, I went next-door for a drink and partied with Willie Nelson. What a sweet, kind man. He was in town when Merle Haggard played at The Saddle Rack. That was a great concert. I met a few of the boys in the band that night. I was really into the party scene back then. I remember going to the West Palm Beach Rock Festival and drinking Southern Comfort with Janis Joplin in an elevator. I hung out with "Big Brother and the Holding Company" by the pool at the hotel where they filmed the T.V. game show, "Treasure Island." The Rolling Stones played, but I never met them. Mick Jagger could really move, though.

I was never a groupie, I just always happened to be in the right place at the right time. My first boyfriend was the bass player from Grand Funk Railroad. Mel Schacher was a real sweetheart. Shy, kind and gentle. Then I dated Greg Lake from Emerson, Lake and Palmer a few times. Lots of guys. The good old days. Sex, drugs and rock n roll. Thank God, He stepped in and changed my life, there is really no comparison between my old life and the one I have now!

I guess one of my big chances to be famous occurred while I was at the LeBaron Hotel. One day, two gentlemen came in to the restaurant. I walked over to their table and said, "Hi, how are you today?"

"Just fine, just fine."

"How would you like to feel finer? How about a cocktail?"

The one guy got all excited and launched into a sales pitch worthy of Herb Tarlic. He said, "I'm talking Walt Disney! I'm talking movies! I'm talking about getting your voice on tape!! Record anything, just get your voice on tape and send it to me!!"

I thought, "Why not?"

"Cool!" I said.

So the next day, I went down to see my friend Steve. He had a transmission shop called Bullshift Transmission.

"Steve," I said, "I am supposed to get my voice on tape. Can I read a commercial of yours and record it?"

He said, "You write it, and you record it."

So I went home to Valentine Acres to write a commercial. The two-seater outhouse was a great place to think and wait for inspiration to strike.

"Has your transmission gone bonkers?? Does it bump, grind or pop out of gear? You've got troubles! You need to know how to bullshift your way out! Get your rear in gear and call Bullshift!"

I finished it off with some great sound effects of grinding gears and the like, and recorded my first commercial. Unfortunately, once it was all done, I discovered I had lost the guy's number, so my career as a voice artist for Disney went up in smoke. At least Steve made a lot of money from that commercial, and it even made the papers!

"While we were dining at the LeBaron Hotel in San Jose, cocktail waitress Cindy Sanderson was going after a measure of celebrity herself. Hers are those voices you hear on those Bullshift transmission commercials, and anyone who can say that name consistently without having the FCC coming down her neck is bound to become famous!"

In the end, I guess I got my fifteen minutes of fame. The whole experience with

Cindy Sanderson California Girl waitress at Lebaron Hotel

the commercial was quite interesting to me, so the following year, I enrolled in Ron Bailie's School of Broadcasting. I studied radio, television, and broadcasting. I learned the ropes of being weather girl, anchorwoman and how to run camera. I graduated in 1981.

Fame and broadcasting wasn't done with me yet, but it would have to wait awhile. I was about to embark on another adventure.

***

LOST AT SEA

One day, a girlfriend of mine, also named Cindy, asked me if I wanted to go fishing. It was a beautiful, sunny morning and I had the day off work, so I said, "Why not?" Just the thought of fresh fish tickled my appetite. So, we hopped in a sixteen foot skif with her dad and her brother and took off out of Vallejo, California. We wouldn't be gone for much more than an hour, so we just went with the clothes on our back.

We motored pretty far out of sight, looking for a school of fish. I was dreaming of frying up some fish and my mouth was watering. I was ready to catch the big one!

It was good to be so far out and away from the habits of daily life. The sun was on my face, my hair was blowing in the wind and the smell of the sea air was refreshing. The waves slammed against the boat, splashing us with a fine mist of salt water. *I was a free spirit, jumping the waves, I was in another world, at one with nature and at peace with God...*

Right about then, the motor stopped. So much for being at peace. We were dead in the water. We had no tools, no extra supplies, nothing. Our only hope was that someone would come by and help us get the motor going again. But there was not a soul around. Just us and the sea.

 Time went by, the sun went down. The wind kicked up and it started pouring rain. We were way off course, freezing and floating, bobbing like a cork in the endless ocean. We had no food, no water, no nothing. We didn't even have a flashlight. All we had was one hefty trash bag.

The worst thing was no bathroom. Not too bad for the guys, but us girls had to hang our backsides over the edge of the boat. It was a real trick trying to hang on to a wet and slippery boat in the middle of a storm in *that* position. Fortunately, no one was lost and the guys were kind enough to turn around and give us some privacy. No doubt they would have got a much-needed laugh from our predicament.

It was very windy and pouring rain. We had a bucket to hold all the fish that we never caught, so we used it to bail the water out of the bottom of the boat. We later found out that there was a small craft warning out, but I guess we were just in the wrong place at the wrong time. So, we shivered and huddled together for warmth, hoping and praying to be rescued. I was trying to send a message by telepathy to my boyfriend, Michael, but I guess he just didn't hear me. Men. They just *never* listen.

Darkness came. The storm raged all night, all the next day, and through the night again. We floated with nothing to guide us but the hand of God. When the sun finally came up, we saw that the storm had broken. I was so relieved. Then I spotted a helicopter flying around. I grabbed that trash bag and started waving it around like a crazy woman, screaming, "HELP, HELP!!"

They didn't see us and flew right on by. We hung our heads in despair. Several times throughout the day, we saw small planes and helicopters and I kept waving that trash bag. I thought it would make a great commercial. SAVED by a Hefty trash bag! I vowed that I would call them with the idea if I made it home alive.

My arms were sore from waving, and we were all feeling weak from the cold and no food or water. We were beginning to lose hope of ever being rescued. But I was about to learn that prayers work better than telepathy. Michael didn't hear me, but God sure did.

I looked up to see a helicopter coming towards us. A basket was lowered, and one by one, we were pulled up out of the boat. They wrapped us up in blankets and gave us some juice and a candy bar and flew us to firm, dry land. When the helicopter landed, we just literally rolled right out of it.

We couldn't walk. We had been in the fetal position for two days, trying to stay warm. Our rescuers helped us to our feet and got us into a clinic for a checkup. We had hypothermia, but other than that, we were fine.

Michael drove up in his tow truck, and when he saw me, he started crying. He said, "I didn't know whether you were dead or alive!"

I said, "Hon, I would do it all again for the helicopter ride!" I *love* flying in helicopters.

When I returned to work, my boss was going to fire me for not showing up to work and not calling. My girlfriend spoke up and said, "You can't fire her! She was lost at sea for two days! Look! It's even in the paper!!!"

Thank God, He rescued me from being lost at sea and from losing my job! Very soon after, I was chosen out of five hundred people to receive the Employee of the Year Award. I didn't even have to sleep with anyone to get it!

FROM PLAYBOY BUNNY TO BUSH BUNNY

In 1983, I was dating a man named Don. He owned a couple of machine shops in San Jose. I was living up in the redwood forest, the land of the giant trees. Redwood Estates was between San Jose and Santa Cruz. It was beautiful there, but I was restless. The winds of change were calling my name. When Don asked me to move with him to San Francisco and live on his boat, "The Second Wind", I was thrilled. A second wind was just what I needed.

"The Second Wind" was a fifty-foot Columbia sailboat. She was long and sleek, and one of the best boats ever made for the sea. Teakwood, with rich shades of blondes, reds and browns. She was a little fragile and delicate, but she was a classy

The "Second Wind"

lady. With a little polishing and care, she was beautiful.

So, the introduction to my life as a sailor was sanding and polishing teakwood. I guess I was more of a deckhand than a sailor really, but I was *way* cuter than the average deckhand. I was a little thing back then, now I'm *twice* the person I used to be. In the morning I would put on my bikini and go to work. I liked the feel of the hot sun, but it took a little work to get a tan. My fair skin usually just burned at first. Then it would peel. Then the freckles would come out. Then finally, I would be a nice golden brown. Together with my long blonde hair, I looked like a playboy bunny.

Life on a boat was a different world from what we were used to. The boat was on Sierra Parkway, right across from Oyster Point, about a mile away from Candlestick Park. The gentle waves would rock us to sleep and we were awakened in the morning by the sun shining through the porthole.

I would spend hours sitting on the deck, breathing the sea air, and just enjoying God's creation all around me. Pelicans, diving and scooping up fish. It was amazing to watch them fill their bills, then swallow the fish whole. I always wondered if they ever got indigestion.

The otters always brought a smile to my face. Some mornings, they would bang against the boat, almost as if they were saying, " Wake up, wake up, it's a brand new day!"

They are such playful creatures, always flipping and turning and splashing about in the water. Watching them eat oysters and mussels on their bellies was a real joy. The babies would ride on mom's belly, just hanging on and trying to get any morsel of food she might drop. They were so cute!

Seeing the fish jump always made me hungry. There is just nothing like catching a fresh fish and eating it right way. I ate fish for breakfast, lunch and dinner. The ocean was our garden, filled with everything we needed, and it was right at our front door. Maybe that experience was God's way of preparing me for living in Alaska, getting accustomed to being close to nature, and of course, fishing for my supper! It wouldn't be long before I made the leap from playboy bunny to bush bunny…

One day, I was out on deck, in my bikini, sanding and polishing, and trying to prepare my mind to start navigational school. Don and I were having trouble with our relationship and I was starting to wonder what I was doing with my life. We've all been there. I was upset and depressed and in tears. I started thinking about Alaska. I had taken a trip there in the past and had loved it. Before I got involved with Don, I had been saving my money to move there. I had been sidetracked,

but I never forgot my dream of becoming an Alaskan. Don came along and asked why I was crying. I said, " I am ready to move to Alaska."

"When?" he said.

"Now!"

Don thought for a moment. "Cindy," he said, "you have to plan and pack for Alaska. Your birthday is next week, why don't we leave then. I'll go with you and see that you make it safely there. It'll be a fun trip."

I was so happy that Don was willing to help me. "What a good guy." I thought.

So, the next week on August 20th, my birthday, we set sail - we drove actually. It took us three weeks and we had a ball. We stopped in at the San Juan Islands, and then on to Victoria on Vancouver Island where we stayed at the Empress Hotel. The Empress is a fancy old hotel that was built in 1908 and looks like a castle. The Canadian Pacific Railway Company built a chain of these enormous hotels across Canada and they were *the* place to stay for the rich and elite. We were neither rich, nor elite, but we still had fun. The rest of the trip wasn't quite as uptown, but we had a great time, camping and fishing.

After we arrived in Anchorage, I settled in up on Rabbit Creek with Neil and Pat, who were some old friends of mine. Don left to go back to California, and I started my new life. Only a month later, Don called me and said, " I miss you. Would you come home, I have finally realized you are the girl I want to marry."

So, I packed up everything and drove back to California. It was the dead of winter, and I was alone. While traveling through the Yukon, I hit icy patches and spun out three times. I managed to get back on the road, thank God, as there was not a soul in sight to help me. I was off to marry Don. I was so excited; I couldn't wait to get there.

When I finally arrived, Don greeted me with, " You're too

late. I'm getting married on Friday." I was crushed. His first
wife's best friend had just sailed in from the Marques Islands.
He had always had a crush on her, and within a week, he had
proposed to her instead. I was crushed and mad and ready to
kill him. But, Alaska sounded better than prison, so I started
working three jobs to save money to go back north.
I figured I might have better luck finding me a husband in
Alaska. I had heard there were lots of men and lots of money
there. Alaskan men – where the odds are good but the goods
are odd. I didn't know it at the time, but I was destined
to experience the truth in that statement before finding that
elusive husband.
Well, I finally got enough money and booked passage on
the ferry through the Inside Passage so I wouldn't have to
make the long drive by myself again. It was a beautiful ride.
Through southeast Alaska, you sail through lots of islands
and see eagles, seals, killer whales, humpback whales and
dolphins that swim alongside the boat. Rugged mountains
with snow capped peaks, mountain goats climbing to
unimaginable heights, glaciers and lakes, and an ocean full
of fish and plant life. It was such a humbling feeling to take
it all in and think that God almighty could design such a
creation with His breath in only seven days. Alaska. It is an
amazing country that you have to experience for yourself,
and once you do, it gets into your heart and your blood and
your soul.
Finally, I was home!!

***

BALLOONS OVER ALASKA

As February comes to a close and March begins, the town of Anchorage, Alaska comes alive. The Anchorage Fur Rendezvous, known to the locals as Fur Rondy, is ten days of uniquely northern events and activities that range from the serious to the outrageous.

The tradition of the Anchorage Fur Rendezvous dates back to the early 1900's, when the miners and trappers emerged from the wilderness to socialize and trade their furs. There were competitions in survival skills and prizes were awarded for the best fox, longest fox and finest ermine pelts.

Today, the festival includes a number of events that have very little to do with fur, and a lot to do with getting a little crazy and shaking off cabin fever. Opening night boasts a fireworks display and then the games begin. The Frostbite race, snowshoe baseball, and indoor games and competitions that include Judo, basketball, tennis and curling. With further entertainments like the Native Musical, the Eskimo blanket toss and an outdoor public auction, there is always something to see!

The world champion sled dog races are always a big highlight of the local activities, then you can head over to the carnival and take in a few rides before catching the parade and the running of the reindeer. Top that off with the bagpipe competition, international dance festival, a polka festival and the formal Fur Rondy Masked Ball, cabin fever just doesn't stand a chance!!

It brings the community together to celebrate the end of a long, long winter. Fur Rondy is now one of the largest winter festivals in North America, and boy is it fun!!

The first year I was in Alaska, I lived in Anchorage. I went to check out the festival with longtime friends, Pat and Neil.

We had a great time. There actually wasn't enough snow that year, so they had to bring some in to downtown for the sled dog races. Everywhere you looked, there were races, food stands, ice sculptures and fun events.

I decided I wanted to fly in the Hot Air Balloon Races so I signed up and met my team. There must have been about twenty-five balloons in that race. Our balloon was called "The Hot Air Affair". It was just beautiful and so colorful!

We had the balloon laying on its side so we could fill it up, but our first setback, the propane torch caught the balloon on fire and burned part of it. Fortunately, it didn't do too much damage. We decided it was safe enough to fly, so all four of us piled into the little wicker basket and away we went.

It was an incredible experience. You get a whole different view of the scenery from way up in the sky. Floating above the town, surrounded by snow capped mountains and twenty-five colorful balloons with the ocean glistening far below. The sky was bright blue and the only sound in the cold, crisp air was the *woosh* of the propane heat rising up into the balloon.

It was a humbling experience. You realize just how tiny you are in comparison to God's magnificent creation, but being tiny and humble among the majestic mountains is still exhilarating. I didn't want it to end. I

Cindy, Furs & Handsome Trappers!
Fur Rondy Anchorage, Alaska

could've just kept going and sailed away over the horizon to far away lands. But, too soon it was over and we had to come back down to earth.

We landed to discover that we had come in last. We cracked open a bottle of champagne and toasted our magical ride in the "Hot Air Affair". In a way, we were the winners. Being last, we had spent more time than anyone else flying free, high above the city. Yes, placing last in the balloon races at Fur Rondy is a memory I will always cherish.

***

Memories of "The Hot Air Affair"
Photo courtesy of Hugh McLellan

ALASKAN WINTERS

There are three seasons in Alaska. Winter, breakup, and summer.

Breakup is when winter tries to turn into spring and everything is half frozen and sloppy. It does not mean a person is broke up (i.e. injured) or that two people have broken up (i.e. ended their relationship) although these two situations do sometimes occur during breakup.

Then there's summer for two weeks, followed by pre-winter. On Halloween, you design a costume that will fit over your snowsuit so you can go trick or treating in a blizzard. The first day of moose season is a national holiday. Everyone celebrates by trying to narrow down their favorite ten moose recipes to a first choice.

There are lots of advantages in having a long winter. Driving is better because the pot holes get filled up with snow, you can see this clearly through the floor boards of your pickup truck. You can just leave your Christmas lights up all year round. Mine have been up for *years*. In my opinion, it makes up for the few small negative things, like having more mileage on your snow blower than your car, or owing more money on your snow machine than you owe on your car.

Winter in Alaska is fantastic, once you learn to prepare properly for it. Sexy lingerie is essential - fleece socks and flannel nightie are always in style, the nightie with the buttons up the front is the obvious choice; they are easier to get on over the moose hide blanket for those chilly nights when the mercury dips down to minus seventy.

A great choice for footwear is bunny boots. No, they are not for bunnies, and *no*, they are not made of bunnies. They were designed for the military. They make your feet look gigantic, but will keep your feet warm and dry, even if they get wet on the inside.

One of the best things about winter (that is, if you are prepared) is the food. Moose, caribou, bear, and smoked fish. The freezer is stuffed full with so many choices. Game meat, pink salmon, red salmon, king salmon (my favorite), smoked salmon, halibut, shrimp, or king crab. That's living off the land and the sea for you! Not a hardship, but a blessing here in the land of plenty!

The land here provides more for us than just food. Every year, we get something called a Permanent Fund Dividend, which is residuals from the oil pipeline out of Prudhoe Bay. We get paid just for living here! Hey, someone has to!

I remember one year, I actually put up with the pain of a toothache until I got my PFD check in October. Another year, my boyfriend and I took a Hawaiian vacation with our checks. While walking down the beach, we passed a beautiful woman in a bikini. My boyfriend said, "Boy, I'd sure like to see her in a snowmobile suit!"

Kristal, Trinity & Kirk Jr. Wilson
snow machining in Glennallen, Alaska

I personally have a grizzly bear thong bikini, and in the summer I wear it while I run, growling, through the sprinkler. It's the closest I ever get to the bare, uh, bear outdoors!

* * *

Danyka Johnson Taste Testing Moose Jerky
A True Child of The North!
Photo by Linda Johnson

"There's no place like home on a cold winter day!"
Photo by Kristal Wilson

STRANDED IN AN ESKIMO VILLAGE

It was a cold winter morning in Gakona. I had just arrived from Valdez. The temperature was minus forty and I was hung over. Those were the B.C. days of my life, (before Christ) and I partied a lot.

The night before, I had almost married a guy I had known from Valdez. His name was Big Jim, and at one time he was the president of the Brother's Biker Club in Fairbanks. I generally don't date bikers, as I can barely ride a pedal bike, let alone hang on to someone going ninety miles an hour on a Harley. I'm more of a bush pilot and gold miner type of gal.

So there I was, at my friend Howard's house. It was so cold that I could see my breath, so I stoked up the fire and decided that this was a Bloody Mary morning. Mary in hand, I fixed some nachos, and said a silent prayer of thanks to God for not letting me marry Big Jim. I had just settled in to watch a movie when the phone rang.

It was another old friend. Dallas is a chiropractor and, at the time, he had a practice in Dillingham. I hadn't seen him in eight months or so. He lived about two hours away and had already heard I was in the area. Word gets around fast in rural Alaska.

"Hey, what are ya doin?" he asked.

"I almost got married to a biker dude last night." I replied.

"You don't do biker guys," he said.

"I know, so I'm here, hanging out with Bloody Mary. "

In retrospect, I realized it was the perfect time for springing something on me.

"How about coming to an Eskimo village with me and working for me? "

"Doing what?" I asked.

"You can run my office and learn how to do massage."

I thought for a moment. "When?" I asked, hoping he meant in about a month, which would give me just about enough time to recover.

"Can you leave now?"

I was stunned. Certainly he didn't mean right this second. Still in shock, I made the mistake of opening my mouth and heard myself say, "OK. See you soon."

I hung up the phone and wondered not only what I had gotten myself into, but also if I had gone mad, narrowly escaping marriage to move to an Eskimo village. Oh well, not being married, I was free as a bird, and, I had to admit, ready for a new adventure.

I met up with Dallas. We picked up a six-pack of beer and headed for Anchorage to catch the next flight to Dillingham. My new home.

I sure got around back then. Sometimes I kind of miss flying around by the seat of my pants and moving here and there. I guess I must have a touch of gypsy in me…

Dillingham is 327 miles southwest of Anchorage, right off the Bering Sea. It's got a highly mixed population of Inuit, Aleuts, First Nations and Caucasians. Primary activities are commercial fishing, fish processing, cold storage and support of the fishing industry. Many residents depend on trapping beaver, otter, mink, lynx and fox to provide cash income. The local diet consists largely of salmon, grayling, pike, moose, bear, caribou and berries. The only way in is by air or sea.

A town full of hard working fisherman is the place to be for a chiropractor and a masseuse. Dallas had just bought a run down old building. It needed a lot of work. I had wondered what I was getting myself into, I was about to find out. Dallas wanted me to tile the floor and the ceiling. The drywall was ready to be sanded too, so that was added to my list of chores. Then came organizing his office and performing my secretarial duties while learning to be a masseuse. In my spare time, I had to clean an apartment upstairs. It was full of cat hair. I am highly allergic to cats, so when I was done, I got to see the local hospital. My list of chores was endless, but it certainly got my mind off my narrow escape from the bonds of matrimony.

In February, Dillingham has a festival called "Beaver Round Up". There is a parade on Main Street and lots of activities all around the town. The bars have music; there are food stands everywhere and lots of crafts for sale. Everyone gets together to shake off their cabin fever and celebrate that spring is near. Dallas showed me a good time and I figured that it seemed like a pretty fun place to be.

When he left town a few days later, he forgot to leave me any money. I had ten dollars to my name. I thought, "What am I going to do now?"

I went to the store and bought three TV dinners and put them in the snow bank, as the old house had no refrigerator. I was going to ration myself and make the three dinners last for one month. I had no choice. The next day, I went outside to get one for lunch and they were all gone. Vanished. Nothing left but shreds of cardboard. A dog had found my cache. I could see him running away with a happy, happy face.

I was bummed out, to say the least. I was hungry and cold and wondered what the heck I was going to do. But, I needn't have worried. The next day, I went across the street to the Bristol Inn and got a job bartending and waitressing. I even got a meal with my shift, *way* better than TV dinners. Now, *that* was a real blessing!

∗∗∗

LIVING IN A TENT
AND SKINNING A BEAR

Before settling down in Skagway, I lived the life of a gypsy, roaming wild and free around Alaska. I recall one winter spent working at a lodge located right on Lake Louise. We were about three hours north of Anchorage, in the interior of Alaska. It's really off the beaten path, out in the middle of nowhere. Rugged, but very beautiful. It has to be for people to tolerate temperatures that stay between minus fifty and minus seventy for most of the winter!

The lodge I was working at was called the Point of View Lodge. There were two other lodges in the vicinity and summer cabins scattered throughout the woods and on the islands. It was kind of neat, our own little community in the bush, population: 88.

We had lots of fun and there was always something to do. We had dances, went dog sledding, played on snow machines and held poker runs. In the summer, there was lots of boating and fishing to keep us busy. It could be a real hopping place, but we had our share of quiet times too. I liked it; it was the best of both worlds.

Of course, we had to take time out of all that fun to do *some* work. I was a versatile gal, my duties were bartending, serving, as well as cleaning the rooms in the lodge and three cabins. The guy who ran the place was a German fellow named Wolfgang. He was pretty nasty and ornery, and would often steal my tips. He cooked a big turkey at Thanksgiving, but refused to give me any dinner. I was *starving*, so later on I snuck into the kitchen to get a turkey leg out of the fridge. But he caught me and yelled at me until I started to cry.

Well, I had had enough, so I quit. I headed down the road a few miles to the Wolverine Lodge and they hired me right on the spot. I often wondered if they were accustomed to hiring people who were fed up with ole Wolfgang's shenanigans.

I settled into a log cabin with an outhouse. One night it was really cold, probably around seventy below, and the outhouse was a bit too far away for my comfort, so I just went around out back of the cabin. It was a full moon and it would have been a fine night to enjoy the scenery, but that cold gets rather nippy on bare skin, so I was in a hurry.

There I was, my warm breath steaming around me, my pants around my ankles, the moon shining brightly, a perfect postcard. I sensed something out of the ordinary, though, and looked up to see an enormous moose. His face was about a foot away from mine and he was staring intently at me, no doubt wondering what the heck I was doing, crouched, half naked in the snow at seventy below.

I screamed and bolted for the cabin. How I made it to the cabin without breaking a leg, I'll never know, as in my haste, I hadn't bothered to deal with my clothing. Nope, I was floundering through the snow, pants around my ankles, going hell bent for leather for that cabin door.

Fortunately the moose, no doubt blinded by the moonlight shining off my bare backside, or perhaps paralyzed by laughter, didn't attempt to follow me into the cabin. He could have quite easily trampled me. They can be very dangerous animals, especially if they have young nearby. It is not unheard of for people to get attacked by moose if they happen to be in the wrong place at the wrong time, which I clearly was.

Back in the warm cabin, I breathed a sigh of relief and said a brief prayer, thanking the Lord for sparing me from being trampled out in the snow and the cold. I also made a promise to myself to equip my little cabin with a honey bucket to avoid placing myself in any further compromising situations.

Yes, it was a full and busy winter. Besides communing with nature, I decided to learn how to cross country ski. One sunny day, when the thermometer reading was about minus fifty, I strapped on a pair of skis and went down to the frozen lake all the way to the boat ramp. I almost froze to death. I sold my skis shortly after. I guess I should have tried it on a warmer day. I may have enjoyed it more and decided against giving it up completely. Oh well, such is life.

It had been a long cold winter, and finally spring was on its way. I was so happy when it started to warm up and the snow started to melt. It got very muddy and sloppy and signs of warmer days ahead began to appear.

I was sitting in the Lodge, having a cup of tea and thinking about what I should do for the coming summer. I was ready for a change. Just then, the satellite phone rang and as I was the only one around, I put down my mug of tea and went to answer it. It was a gal wondering if there were any Lodge employees looking for summer work. I got all the details and asked when the job started.

"Tomorrow." she said.

I thought about it for a moment and said, "I'll take it!"

I told my boss that I had a new job and would be leaving. As things were pretty slow at that point and her sister had decided to come and help her out, they could do without me.

I packed my gear up and headed for Anchorage that afternoon. The job was in the middle of Alaska, south of McGrath, at an exclusive fishing and hunting lodge called Stony River Lodge. I met Jim, the owner, the next afternoon in Anchorage. We loaded up all the gear and groceries into an Otter bush plane, and away we went.

Twenty four hours after drinking tea and wondering what I should do for the summer, here I was in a bush plane, flying through enormous mountains into the heart of a rugged and unforgiving land, to start my new job. Only in Alaska! When we had officially reached the middle of nowhere, we finally landed at the camp. It was right on the Stony River. It may have been unforgiving territory, but it was certainly stunning. God's masterpiece, and no one to see it for hundreds of miles around, except me and the other lucky campers.

The lodge was simple, but nice. It had a big kitchen and dining room, and a loft upstairs for the chef. We were catering to the elite, offering hunting and fishing tours. For twenty thousand dollars, you could hunt moose, bear, caribou and sheep, all in one trip. The sheep was the toughest, a person needed to be really fit to climb those high mountains. One guest was Bela Karolyi, coach of Olympic medalist Mary Lou Retton. He was a great guy and a lot of laughs. We always enjoyed having him in camp.

My job kept me pretty busy. Besides assisting the chef as prep cook, I had to clean the cabins, living room and library area, stack firewood, and generally keep the place looking nice. I planted some flowers and made some rock gardens. I did get some time off in the afternoons, so I fished a lot. You can only eat so much fish though, so I would smoke some of it. Most northerners love smoked fish better than candy, and I'm no exception!

One of the fishing and hunting guides was a bush pilot, and he had a Super Cub. They are great little planes that can get right down close to the areas you want to look at. Sometimes we could even spot wolf and bear tracks, we could get that close. I love flying, so it was a great way to spend free time. One day we saw a huge grizzly chasing a big bull moose at about 35 miles per hour. It was absolutely amazing to watch from the air. The wilds of Alaska, the last frontier! It has always been exciting to me, and after all these years, I still love living here.

The season was in full swing and we were booked full. We had clients from all over the world; it was fascinating to meet them all. Some of them had saved all their lives to come on this trip, it was their dream come true. It was hard work, but there were lots of laughs and good times, too.

One day, I told my boss that I didn't feel very important just being a dishwasher and cleaning lady. The next day, he sent the chef on a bear hunt, and I became the head chef! Dream come true! But could I do the job?

My first dinner, I made caribou spaghetti, and I burned it. I had to serve 30 people that night, and I couldn't even eat it. I remembered hearing about a trick where you put baking soda to take the burnt smell away. So, I dumped in quite a bit of baking soda, actually, almost the whole box, and what do you know? They loved it! Baking soda, the magic ingredient!! I breathed a sigh of relief. Once again, the Lord had come to my rescue.

I guess my good cooking must have smelled pretty good because it started to attract bears. I was alone a lot while the guys were out hunting and fishing, and it was pretty scary. I would run into the lodge for refuge and then peek my head out through the window and watch the bears get into the barbecue and come onto the porch looking for any scraps we might have left behind. Once they start coming around, they just don't stop and they can be a real problem.

One night, as I lay fast asleep, one of the guides came and woke me up.

"Hey Cindy! We got the bear and we need your help skinning it."

I thought there would be no better way to get over my fear of bears. We put our headlamps on and the guys taught me how to do it properly so I wouldn't ruin the hide. It was a big job, but finally we were done and the next morning we bagged up all the meat. My last day in camp, the boys fixed me bear heart for breakfast. It was pretty tasty!

They said I made camp life a lot of fun, and as a parting gift, they gave me the bear hide. I worked at Stony River Lodge for two summers. I sure learned a lot about the wilderness and made some great friends. Indeed, I did leave my heart at Stony River.

I will never forget the experience of living in a tent and skinning out a bear.

***

Kirk Wilson, Alaskan Hunter and Grizzy Bear

Kirk & Julie Wilson "Toasting The Hunt!"

VALDEZ OIL SPILL

When the season had ended at Stony River Lodge, I was ready for a change. My stint as head chef had started my creative juices flowing, and I was hungry to pursue my career in broadcasting. I called some old friends from Santa Cruz, California, they told me to come on down.

So, back to the lower 48. Santa Cruz is a beautiful place, right on the ocean. Lisa and Lou had an enormous home and they kindly opened their doors to me. It was beautiful.

I went from living in a wall tent in the wilds of Alaska to the lap of luxury. I had a huge heart-shaped brass bed and a bathroom the same size as my tent had been. At this point, running water and electricity were a real treat for me, but there was also a shower, jacuzzi tub, and best of all, a flush toilet. No more outhouses for this gal! I was in heaven.

When I arrived that year, Lou was working at Santa Cruz Film-Making Production Studios. He was the Senior Vice President of audio production. I had been friends with him and Lisa for years, and whenever I would visit, Lou and I would make up commercials just for fun. He always thought I had talent and a nice radio voice. With my broadcasting school under my belt, he thought I would be a good addition to the team.

I started work at the Santa Cruz studios. I was the receptionist and general one-woman welcome-wagon for anyone who came through our doors. I also did in-house talent. I did several voice-overs for television and radio. I loved it. The studios had a film production team, television, video and audio room, postproduction, producers and directors, equipment rentals, a sound stage, creative services and a talent department.

The people who worked there were real professionals, but

they were a lot of fun too. I lived and worked there for six months. It was fascinating work and we had a lot of laughs, but I was missing Alaska. Fancy cars and fancy clothes were just not my style anymore. Alaska was in my blood and I felt like a fish out of water.

Then news came of the oil spill in Valdez. My heart sank. I felt a yearning to get back home and help in some way. The devastation of the whole thing made me sad and heartsick. I finally made the decision to go home. I gave my two weeks notice and started packing.

The studios closed down the whole place and threw a big party for me in Capitola at the Edgewater bar and grill, whom I had once done a commercial for. It meant so much to me that the studios had appreciated me and wanted to give me such a great send off. I would miss it all, but I had to go home. After the party, I hit the road. Alaska or Bust.

It was a long drive to Alaska. I finally arrived in Valdez. It was a mess. There was oil everywhere. The land, the sea life, the animals, everything covered in oil. It was just so sad to see.

The town was booming though, full of hard working people, working as fast as they could to set things right. I went straight to the Club Bar for a beer. I needed it after the drive and I have found that bars usually know what the scoop is and who's hiring.

The bartender came to take my order, and lo and behold, it was a gal I had worked with in another town. June and I really hit it off, and then I ran into Patti, another old friend from further north. June offered me a job as a cocktail waitress at the bar and Patti invited me to live with her on a boat called "The Outlaw". God was taking care of me. He always does, although sometimes we don't realize it. Five minutes, and I had a job and a place to live. Now that's some fancy footwork!

The Club Bar was right on the harbor, so I could just walk

straight up the ramp and I was at work. At the time, it was the rowdiest bar in the United States. We averaged five fights every night. It was always packed, and I was the only cocktail waitress. I got to know everyone who came in. The first two guys I met at the Club Bar were Mike Korsmo and Tim Roseberg. They were living in Skagway at the time but were working the Valdez oil spill on boats helping with the clean up. They were great guys and a bundle of laughs and always brought a smile to my face when I saw them at work. Little did I know that later on we would be living in the same town here in Skagway. Funny how life goes.

One night, I had about ten guys come in and say, "Cindy, we are going to go out and clean rocks and animals for three months. When we come back, we'll give you a fifty to one hundred dollar tip if you can remember our names."

So, while they were gone, I worked on memorizing their names. When they returned, I greeted all ten of them by name, and I got my fifty-dollar tip. I made good money remembering people's names, but I also realized how important it is to remember someone's name. Everybody likes to be remembered by name. Don't you?

Now, when I do my tours in Skagway, I learn up to sixty names in ten minutes. Everyone is VIP to me. Remembering names is a gift from God; I think He gave it to me so I could touch peoples' hearts.

That summer was a wonderful experience. Keeping the workers happy was my part in the big clean up. I loved living on the "Outlaw". Patti and I had dinner parties and ate lots of smoked fish, and we were never without a date. We were very popular. Not that we were without our charms, but there were very few gals around, so that helped out a bit.

That winter, I decided to move off the boat. It was just getting too darned cold. And just in time. Very shortly after I left, the "Outlaw" sank. Thank God, there was no one on board at the time.

I moved into a trailer out by the dump, but it froze up. I had started dating a fellow who lived in a big old warehouse, so I moved in with him and his brother for the winter. We had 550 inches of snow that year. Driving through town was like being a mouse in a maze. It would dump five feet of snow in a night and the next morning we would get another five feet. We were constantly shoveling to be able to get to and from work, and then more shoveling snow off the roof. For all our efforts, the roof on the warehouse collapsed one night, and we had to evacuate in the middle of a blizzard.

Thank God a friend of mine named Venita rented me a room for the rest of the winter. I was so grateful to finally have a home that was safe. I had had my share of unstable living conditions that winter. I was thankful to be alive and warm.

Praise the Lord!

Valdez Harbor & Club Bar
Photo by Roger Kulstad

STUCK TO THE OUTHOUSE SEAT
AT SEVENTY BELOW

After the Valdez spill, I went back to roaming. I spent a couple years bouncing back and forth across Alaska before I finally landed in Glennallen. Glennallen is in the Interior of Alaska, about three and a half hours north of Anchorage. I was working at a fishing and hunting lodge called Tolsona Lake Resort. Located on beautiful Tolsona Lake, which means, "muddy waters" in the native language, it was quiet and serene. And in the bush.

When an Alaskan says "in the bush", it means that the "bush" is pretty much in the middle of nowhere. This bush was definitely in the middle of nowhere, although the trees weren't very big due to the permafrost. We would see herds of caribou, moose, bears, and river otters playing in the lake while the fish jumped around them. In the winter, we would ice fish for burbot, which tastes like fresh water lobster. One time, I caught a ten-pound lake trout. It took me three days to eat it. *Yum...*

It brought a smile to my face seeing the wildlife roam about. Fortunately, they didn't know they could wind up being our dinner, so they were pretty relaxed. It was their territory, and we just happened to be there. There was lots of space and forest for us to share. But, sometimes the people and the critters cross paths and it creates a bit of excitement.

One day, Kirk, the owner, had been out moose hunting. He was successful, and had hauled the moose home in his plane. There was a big grizzly that had been messing around in the garbage. Once bears get into your garbage, they will just keep coming back and causing problems. There is no changing their minds, and when they decide to hang around, they are really dangerous. Well, **Griz** was hanging around that night. When he smelled the moose blood, he became more interested in the plane than the garbage. The plane was right outside Kirk's bedroom, so he was at very close range. Kirk managed to take care of the bear before too much damage was done. As soon as that bear had started nosing in the garbage, his days were numbered, and that night he got a one-way ticket to the big garbage dump in the sky.

Kirk and his wife, Julie, were good friends of mine. They had owned the lodge for twenty-five years. People came for weekend getaways to relax in the peace and quiet, enjoy the fishing, or play on snowmobiles. Weary travelers would also stop for the night, and sometimes there were crews that were working on the pipeline. There were six motel rooms, and a restaurant with excellent food, especially when Julie and Sharon were cooking. The prime rib was out of this world; it would just melt in your mouth. I can still taste it…

Both the bar and the restaurant overlooked the lake. The bar was big, with room for couches and a pool table. Kirk was an avid hunter and fisherman and the evidence was plainly seen throughout the lodge. There was a buffalo, a mountain goat, a caribou, a moose (just the heads), a good size walrus, and a wolverine.

It was a beautiful place and I loved working there. I had gone there for a drink and stayed for three days. Then they hired me. I had bartended a lot in Alaska, where it's light all summer, dark all winter, and the bars are open until 5 A.M. You just never know who will show up in the wee hours of the morning when you are out in the bush.

I lived in a small one- room cabin right on the lake. Before I got my outhouse, I knew which leaves were good toilet paper, that is, in the summer time. For my birthday, I got an outhouse and I was thrilled to death. My birthday is in August, but it was a late present, so it was "up and running" that winter. In the winter, it's a good idea to keep a honey bucket in your cabin if you don't have indoor plumbing. Really, who wants to run to the outhouse at seventy below?

For you southerners, a honey bucket is a bucket, but there's no honey in it. The "modern" Alaskan bush woman's chamber pot. Got it?

Anyways, back to my new outhouse. Kirk and Bruce had done a fantastic job. They had carved out a half moon on the side to let the sun and moonlight in, and the smelly air *out.* I had painted it light blue inside and decorated it with words of inspiration and beautiful happy pictures. There was a coffee can with a lid to keep my toilet paper clean and safe from busy little critters on the lookout for nesting material, and a pretty little bowl with a bottle of sanitizer sitting in it. All this topped off the brand spanking new plywood seat. It was a thing of beauty.

Well, the first night I used my new outhouse, it was seventy below. I was hoping it would be a quick trip, and then back into my cozy cabin. But NOOOOO. At seventy below, my brand new plywood seat was just plain frozen wood. And when my warm parts touched that frozen wood, well, you can imagine what happened. Yup. The first time I used my new outhouse, I froze to the seat.

It was a very frightening experience. I was scared and started yelling, but everyone was all tucked up in bed, so no one heard me. After hyperventilating for a moment or two, I caught my breath and prayed really hard to the Lord to HELP me, *quick*! I was literally freezing my butt off! Out of nowhere, I heard a voice say, *" Pee on yourself"*. I took the sanitizer out of the little bowl so I had something to catch it in, and then poured it onto my left butt cheek. PRAISE THE LORD, it worked! Who says God doesn't speak to us. That time, I listened and it did the trick. Glory to God!!

It felt good to be free. I ran back into my cozy lil' log cabin and stood by the wood stove to thaw out my backside. Once it was warm and toasty, I crawled into bed and had a good giggle about what had just happened.

The next day, I went to the hardware store and bought a

deluxe Styrofoam seat so I would have a warm seat the next time it reached seventy below. Well, let's just say it wasn't cold. We have so much to be thankful for in the bush!

✳✳✳

"Home Sweet Home"
Photo by Kristal Wilson

"My Outhouse!"
Photo by Kristal Wilson

"All the Comforts"
Photo by Kristal Wilson

UFO SIGHTING

One snowy night just before Christmas, I closed up the bar and started walking back to my log cabin. Trotting by my side was Willow, a big black Newfoundland dog. She belonged to a friend of mine, but I loved looking after her. She was a real sweetie and great company.

It was snowing really hard; the air was filled with big fluffy snowflakes. Willow's fur was covered and so was my hat and coat. Through the snow, I could just make out Bessie's house.

Bessie owned the lodge for years before selling it to Kirk and Julie. But now, Bessie's health was failing and she needed assistance twenty-four hours a day. Julie, her daughter Kristal, Sharon and I would all take shifts. She lived close by my cabin, so I passed by every night on my way home.

As I got closer, Bessie's house got clearer, as if there was a bright spotlight shining on it. Then I realized there *was* a light over her house. I stopped and looked again. Sure enough. Bright, white light. I thought for sure that the Lord had sent His angels to bring Bessie home. It was late, and Bessie was in good hands, so I didn't stop. As I trudged past her house through the deep snow, I said a prayer for peace and rest for Bessie.

As I rounded the corner of my cabin and headed for the door, I saw a bright neon green light shaped like an oval shining down on Moose Lake, the next lake over. I was tired, and after another quick glance, I figured the guy down at the end of the lake must've had his generator going.

I headed inside, put some music on and started peeling off my many layers of winter clothes. As the warmth penetrated my frozen brain, the image of that green light came back to me. Something wasn't right. It was shining *down* on the lake. That was no generator.

I put all my gear back on and Willow and I headed out to see what the heck was going on. I knew it wasn't northern lights, because they only come out on cold clear nights. I hadn't been drinking. Maybe I was hallucinating?? I felt restless and unsettled. I hadn't seen anything like it before.

With Willow by my side for moral support, I walked down the frozen lake for a stretch before coming to a standstill. The light was the size of a football stadium and it had a stream of white light coming out the top. It was so bright, it hurt my eyes to look at it.

Sharon had lived on Tolsona Lake for over twenty years, and swore she had seen UFO's in the past. Well, now I believed her. I thought to myself, " I have *got* to go and wake her up, she has to see this."

I headed back to the cabin and grabbed my car keys. I would go get Sharon and we would drive to the end of the lake to see what this thing was all about. As I went out the door, I glanced at the clock. Fifty minutes had passed.

Back outside, I looked into the sky and it was dark. No light, nothing. There had been no noise at all. It was just *gone*. After watching a bit longer, I reluctantly went back inside and crawled into bed. I couldn't sleep though. Instead of angels coming to get Bessie, it seemed there were aliens looking us over. I sure hoped they weren't after me!

The next day, I went to spend the weekend with a friend. Sandy lives in Chitna, a few hours away, so on the way I stopped in for a quick visit with my pal Randy. I sat down and told him about the weird lights I had seen the night before. His eyes got really big as I told the story. When I had finished, he said quietly, "I saw the same thing last night."

He had gone outside to see what was up when he had heard some dogs barking. Flying through the canyon was a huge green oval shape with bright lights shining out of it. It was going really fast, but made no noise at all. He said it was almost too bright to look at.

Randy lived two hours away from me, but we both saw the same thing. What was it? It was unexplainable. Randy and I both believe it was a UFO. Are there beings from another world watching us? Knowing that I wasn't alone was a relief. It meant I wasn't crazy, and that maybe "they" weren't chasing me after all. Maybe they were after Randy instead.

Or, maybe aliens get cabin fever, too, and to relieve the boredom, they take a little cruise down to Alaska to watch us crazy northerners. Better than a drive-in movie, you have to admit. And with any luck, we're just a little too wacky for them to consider kidnapping us. See? Being a wild northern woman really does have benefits that you probably never could have imagined! I'm way too much of a handful for a little runt like E.T.!!

THE DOG THAT BIT ME AND DIED

One hot summer day, my boyfriend and I decided to go out to the country on our dirt bike. We packed a picnic basket, grabbed a couple gold pans and our fishing rods, and away we went. This was all new territory to us, so we just went wherever the warm breeze took us.

It was so beautiful that day. Blue skies, soft and fluffy clouds that looked like enormous cotton balls; I wished I could just climb up on one and float away. Soaking up the warm sun, my long hair blowing in the breeze, the whole experience was a gift from God and I was enjoying every minute of it. I didn't have a care in the world and I was free as a bird. We took our time, meandering along. The winding road took us through a forest of spruce and pine. The smell of the evergreens and wildflowers was just heavenly. Squirrels collecting pinecones scampered about and there were monarch butterflies everywhere. Deer casually watched as we cruised past. Nature is certainly God's masterpiece at work.

Down a rough road, we spotted a rustic old miner's cabin. Many years of heavy snows had taken their toll; it was in a pretty sad state. There were rusty old cans of beans and beer cans lying around, looked like quite a diet to me. But, there was a beautiful creek with a perfect spot beside to lay out our picnic blanket, so we decided it was time to eat. Then we could get down to the serious business of fishing and gold panning.

All of a sudden, this crazy man came charging out from under the bridge, screaming at the top of his lungs. "Hey, you, get off my claim!"

His face was distorted with anger. His clothes were tattered, he had a long scruffy beard, and he was really dirty. We brought the bike to a screeching halt, startled to see anyone around out here. We hadn't planned on claim jumping.

Out of nowhere came this little black Chihuahua type dog. He ran straight at me, barking and yapping. I never saw such little legs run so fast. He jumped at me and bit my leg. I had shorts on, so I could plainly see when the blood started to trickle down my leg. I had big boobs back then, well, bigger than they are now for sure. I looked down over my big nuggets, and the dog was lying upside down with his legs straight up in the air. Stiff as a board! *Dead.* That yappy little dog had bit me and *died.* It was so surreal, I felt like I was in some weird cartoon. I just could not believe what was happening.

The old miner started moving away from me, eyes as big as saucers. "Who are you?" he asked. He seemed to think I was a witch or something like it.

I said, "Has your dog had his shots?"

He never did answer me, but he was so rattled by the whole thing that he let us go across the bridge upstream from his dredge where we caught some fish and even found a few flakes of gold. When it was time to leave, I said, "Thanks for everything, and sorry about your dog."

As we drove off into the sunset, I shook my head, wondering if anyone would believe this tale. The first time I ever went gold panning, *a dog bit me and died.* Have <u>you</u> had your shots yet?

OFF TO SKAGWAY
FOR MADAM LESSONS

One night, while I sat with Bessie, the temperature hit seventy below. While she slept, I sat and watched the northern lights dance. They were a symphony in red, green and purple, amazing shapes that were constantly changing. You could even hear them crackle in the atmosphere. It was like God was putting on a fabulous light show just for me. And looking back, I think maybe He was. I didn't know it, but He was about to change my life.

With Bessie still asleep, I decided to call my friend, Jan Wrentmore. She lives in Skagway and owns the Red Onion Saloon.

Now, the Red Onion Saloon was the most exclusive bordello during the Klondike Gold Rush days. In 1898, the building was actually moved from 7th Avenue to near the White Pass Train depot on Broadway, where all the action was. They pulled that whole building by horse and actually pulled it in backwards. Then, they took the front part off the building and moved it to the back, then put the back part on the front. There was a bar and a dancehall downstairs, and cribs for the girls to work out of upstairs. On the back bar, there were 10 dolls, sitting up, each one looking like one of the working girls, or "soiled doves." When the men went upstairs with a girl, they would lie that doll down on it's back. When the man was done with the gal, she would drop the payment down a copper chute in the floor, where it would land on the bar beside the cash register. The bartender would sit the doll back up again, and the next customer would know she was available.

Today the Red Onion Saloon is a bar and restaurant with historical tours given by hostesses playing the part of saloon girls and madams. In the daytime you can hear the music of a Ragtime piano player and different musicians playing in the evenings. One of my favorite bands at the saloon is "Deering and Down". The lovely songstress Lahna Deering and the mystical guitar work of Rev. Neil Down set the mood just right.

As I talked to Jan and watched the northern lights, she hit me with an interesting proposition. "Hey, would you come to Skagway and be my Madam by day and work the Red Onion Saloon at night?"

I said, " Jan, I don't know how to act!"

"You don't have to, " she said, "You're a natural actress!"

The Onion did sound like a fun place to work, so I told Jan I would be down for the season to be her "Madam". So, off I went, to Skagway. It was the summer of 1992.

Skagway, population 835, is also known as "The Gateway to the Klondike." It's a beautiful little town right on the water of the Lynn Canal, the longest, deepest fjord in North America. And I mean little.

The downtown is only 7 blocks long with NO streetlights. The whole town, right to the outskirts, measures only 22 blocks, by 4 blocks wide. There is a post office, a bank and one grocery store, called " The Fairway Market". The food is delivered by barge, once a week, so it's always a bit of relief when it comes in safe and sound. There is one gas station, with high priced gas that has gone from the Alaska pipeline to Seattle to be taxed and then sent back to us. Crazy, huh?

We have a few restaurants and bars in the winter, but in the summer season there are more, because this place is BOOMING with tourists from the cruise ships. Skagway is an important port of call for the cruise ships, as it is the last stop North on the inside passage route.

So it was to this pretty little town surrounded by snow peaked mountains that I arrived to begin my new career. Trouble was, I had never acted before and I had *no* idea how to act like a madam. Now, this was back before I found Jesus, my Lord and Savior. At the time, I was into white witchcraft. I didn't see any harm in it, as it was just good witchcraft. But, "good" witchcraft just leaves the door open for black witchcraft. Take it from me, witchcraft is nothing to be messed with. It is very real and uncontrollable, as I was soon to discover.

I was living in a house called the Bank House on 3rd Avenue and Alaska, with some other employees from the Red Onion. With my then rosy view of witchcraft, I figured, what better way to learn about being a madam than from a madam?"

So I decided to call one up from the spirit world. Well, that house just went *crazy*. Windows and doors were opening and slamming shut. The washer and dryer came on. The water in the sink started running full blast. The TV and stereo came on. I guess they were more interested in all these modern conveniences that they were in helping me. I could literally see all kinds of madams running up and down the stairs, I could hear the pounding of their footsteps, and my heart was pounding right along with them. I was *terrified*. I felt like I was in some bizarre horror movie.

I had no idea how strong and powerful talking to dead spirits would be. I thought my friend Carol was upstairs, and some small part of me was hoping that she was having a wild party and making all the racket, but when I yelled up the stairs, there was no answer. Then I knew I was really alone and that just made it worse.

I ran to the phone. Thankfully, there wasn't a dead madam making a long distance call, so I picked it up and called the Red Onion. Carol answered the phone.

I said, " Carol, I was learning how to be a madam, so I called in a madam from the spirit world and the whole place is *full* of them! I am so scared!"

She said, "Cindabelle, you know better than that! What are you going to do?"

"I'll call my brother," I said. "He can help me."

So, I called my brother Bill in Ohio. "Brother," I said," I called in a bunch of thievin' madams from the spirit world. They are running all over, the house is upside down, everything is crazy! What do I do?"

Bill said, "Light a candle and say, 'In the name of Jesus, everybody leave and get out of here!'"

As soon as I said the name of Jesus *everything* stopped and all the madams were gone. I am so grateful that the Lord Jesus saved the day once again. And that was the last time I had *anything* to do with witchcraft.

I was *very* happy to put that experience behind me, but I still had a problem. I still didn't know anything being a madam. I still thought a madam would be the best teacher, but since the dead ones had been a whole lotta trouble and *no* help at all, I thought maybe I should try talking to a live one. So, I went to have a visit with my neighbor, Big Marge, who had been a madam during the pipeline days. She pulled me into her office and started telling me about the good ole' days. She had cathouses in Valdez and Fairbanks, and had been a very well known and respected Lady of the Evening.

She always told me that I would have been one of her "better" girls. I felt honored to be learning the ropes from a professional.

So began my career as Madam Dolly. During the day I was doing shows at Liarsville, which was owned by Jan at the time. I was also doing brothel tours at the Red Onion Saloon and bartending there at night. I really hit it off with one of the other gals, "Madam Spitfire". (real name – Billi Clem) A few years later we teamed up to put together walking tours of the historic Red Light District and the brothels. We just had a ball.

While I have stayed in entertainment all these years, "Madame Spitfire" went in another direction and is quite the businesswoman. Among other ventures, she opened a children's store called "Alaskan Fairytales". In the back there is another section called "The House of Negotiable Affection" where she sells lingerie and fancy bits and pieces worthy of a madam's boudoir. We are still the best of friends and even in the busy season we still manage to catch up when I stop in at her store to browse for hats and boas to keep Dolly looking her best.

Three miles out of Skagway is the Gold Rush Trail Camp at a place called Liarsville. Although it has a rather unappealing name, it's a beautiful place. In among the cottonwood, spruce and pine trees, a sparkling waterfall trickles down the mountainside. Here starts an old trail that the gold seekers of '98 would climb to hook up with the White Pass Trail. An enterprising journalist (who never made it up the trail) sat by the campfire waiting for miners to return with tall tales that he could write about. That's how Liarsville got its name.

By the time I went to work there, Liarsville boasted tents and cabins furnished with old relics left by the miners, as well as a gift shop. I had learned a script for our show, but rewrote it to suit Madam Dolly. Before my days in Liarsville were over, there was a big outdoor theatre, but when I first started, we just entertained around the campfire and did our best to give everyone a little old fashioned fun with some Gold Rush flavor. Once the performance was over we showed everyone how to pan for gold.

My favorite part of working out at the Gold Rush Trail Camp in Liarsville was seeing Jan's MacKenzie River huskies, Dawson, Trish, Pelly, Teslin, Shandalar and Donjek. Jan also had a giant Alaskan Malamute named Kobuk. They were the stars of the show, Jan's pride and joy, and loved by all. I couldn't wait to get to work to hold the puppies and love them up, and my favorite thing was the smell of their puppy breath.

Jan also had a donkey named Dewey at the camp. Good ole Dewey had a mind all of his own. Every once in awhile he would escape right before showtime just to make sure we were all paying attention to him. On special days, Jan's pot belly pig Georgia would come for a special appearance. She was the sweetest pig I ever met.

We were one big family and so blessed to share in the love of all the animals. I have such fond memories working at Liarsville and I loved my job!

All that singing and entertaining is hard work; we were blessed to get a free meal after the shows. Once the gold pans were hung up, we would cross the road to the Salmon Bake. The salmon was cooked outside on big grills and then served with baked beans, potatoes, coleslaw and apple crisp. I doubt the gold seekers of '98 ever dined so well.

I felt blessed that Jan had asked me to do shows at the Gold Rush Trail Camp in Liarsville. The waterfall made such a peaceful sound. It was paradise. I loved it even when it was pouring rain, the wind was blowing and the mosquitoes were hatching. And those are some big mosquitoes! Any Alaskan will tell you, the mosquito is our state bird!

It would quiet my soul, as I would pray before every show, knowing full well God was always talking to me and guiding my every move. But…. was I listening?

Madam Dolly & Miner Dave at Liarsville

"Madam Dolly" at the Famous Red Onion Saloon!

LIARSVILLE AND MADAM DOLLY'S SURPRISE GUEST

I had a wonderful time working at the Gold Rush Trail Camp in Liarsville; I enjoyed every minute. But, even Madams have their bad days. I remember one particularly rough day. The previous night, my boyfriend and I had gotten into a big fight. I was feeling very depressed and sad. But, the show must go on and an actress has to smile and be happy no matter what. The guests sat on benches around the campfire, eating gingersnaps and sipping apple cider. I managed to finish my performance, but when I came off the stage, I wandered over to the gold panning troughs and I started to cry. I started praying and asking Jesus to take away the pain in my heart and give me something else to focus on so I could be a blessing for someone else. My prayer was answered. At that very moment, a tour bus driver named Julie walked by and said, "Hey Dolly, do you have a moment to go and say hello to a lady on my bus?"

I wiped the tears from my eyes and thanked the Lord for using me to make someone's day. The lady in question was an older woman who was handicapped. She wasn't able to walk around, so she thought she would just wait on the bus until the show was over. I went and said, "Hi, I'm Dolly! It's an honor to meet you! Are you feeling ok? Can I get you some snacks?"

She smiled really big and said, "Yes, that would be great!"

After I brought her some apple cider and gingersnaps, I said, "How about I do a private show just for you, right here on the bus?" She smiled, and I could feel her kind, loving heart. I walked to the back of the bus and entered just as though I was on stage.

"IT'S SHOWTIME!!"

She sipped her cider and munched her gingersnaps, all the while looking as excited as if she had a front row seat at the

Palace Grande Theater.

I said, "Madam Dolly is my name, and mining miners is my game"… and the show began. When I was finished, I gave her a feather from my boa for her bible, and a big hug. She had tears rolling down her cheeks.

She said, "I want to thank you from the bottom of my heart for taking the time to care about an old lady who was unable to walk around. Thank you for bringing me snacks and giving me a private show and for giving me love."

We were crying and hugging. I asked her name and where she was from. Even through her tears, she spoke with eloquence and sophistication. "My name is Louise Alexander, and I used to be an actress. I have traveled and performed all over the world. I have even performed at the Gershwin Theater in New York City, and now you have given *me* a private performance, and for that, I am truly grateful. Thank you, Dolly; you did a wonderful job. You have a golden heart and you have given me a golden moment that will last a lifetime."

We cried and hugged one last time. We stared at each other through the window, until the bus turned and she was out of sight. I had heard later that Louise Alexander had started the first book of acting. I am not sure of that information, but Louise and the Lord gave me a real blessing that day. That moment was priceless, and moments like that are the reason I live to touch peoples' hearts.

I am not an actress; I feel with my heart. If I can just make one person's day and be a blessing, I am happy. I think that if everyone tried to bless just one other person, every day, the world would be a better place. Loving the Lord and touching hearts is my passion; that's what makes Dolly famous. Dolly always says, *"Live your life with passion; expect great things to happen; and remember, the gold is within."*

May God Bless You Always.

***

Dolly at Kid's Tea Party at Mile Zero B&B Skagway
Photo by Tara Mallory

Dawson Dolly at the Klondike Gold Dredge
with the Biggest Nugget in the Klondike!
Photo by Stacy Eaton

H
O
O
T
S

&

T
O
O
T
S

Dolly in front of the original
Steam Engine that took Gold Seekers
over the White Pass

Madam Dolly

Dawson Dolly & Conductor David
Dobbs aboard the White Pass & Yukon
Route RR

Dawson Dolly
White Pass & Yukon Route RR
Parlor Car Hostess

THE MADAM AND THE MINER - TOGETHER AT LAST!

One of the things that really improved in my life when I found the Lord was that I quit dating loser guys. I didn't go out on a date for two years. My life was full, but I was still kind of lonely. I asked the Lord to bring me the right man and trusted that He would when the time was right.

In the meantime, He had given me a busy life in Skagway, filled with wonderful friends.

I was Madam Chaplain at the Eagles Club. The secretary was a good friend of mine, named Will Godbey. Skagway is a small town, so I saw him everywhere. I would see him at church, around town, occasionally we would have lunch or just sit and chat. He also sold gold at Liarsville. Sometimes he would slip me a few nuggets when I came off stage at the end of a show, just like the old days when a miner would slip the Madam a few nuggets. He never did give me his gold poke to hold for safe keeping though. Darn it.

I always thought he was a kind and gentle man. After a lifetime of abusive men, I was really attracted to the idea of spending time with sweet and easy-going types. But, Will was just a pal. After all, I had known him for ten years.

One afternoon, I was at the Eagles Club with some old friends, Red, who is a good friend of mine, and Jay Frey. After agreeing to split the winnings, we settled in for an afternoon of pull-tabs. I was pulling some really high numbers. Will strolled in, just back from gold mining up the creek.

"Hello Will. How are you?" I said.

"Really sick. I have the flu. "

"Well, don't come near me, I've had it three times this summer, and I don't want it again. Go stand over there." I told him.

He stood and watched me as I kept pulling winners. I won

about $500 that night. Will just watched. "She sure is lucky," he said.

It was a magical night. We got together and started dating. When the season ended, we decided to go to Atlin for a week and spend some quality time together. I was excited about meeting some of his miner friends.

We rented a cottage on Atlin Lake. I cooked up a turkey and a ham with all the trimmings and took meals on wheels to the miners up the creek. The air was cool and crisp, the fall colors were spectacular. We had a great time. But a part of me was sad. I had already made plans to move to Glennallen with my sister and the time to leave was getting closer. Will had a few more months of mining, so with a heavy heart, I headed back to Skagway to get ready to leave. We agreed to get together for Christmas.

Winter in Alaska is cold. Temperatures around Glennallen are usually anywhere from thirty to seventy below, but that winter was exceptionally cold. It dropped to around minus fifty or sixty and just stayed there. I was working two jobs and had long distances to drive. I did my best to stay warm and be patient.

Christmas finally arrived and so did Will. He had been traveling for fifteen hours straight, with *no heater.* When he got to our house, his van broke down right where he pulled up. So there he stayed. I was so happy!

At the end of January, he prepared to return to Skagway. More surprises were in store for me. He asked me if I would move back to Skagway and live with him.

"YES!" I said. "I would love to!"

It was fifty-five below when we left that frozen land. It took us three days to get to Skagway because the steering wheel wouldn't turn and the tires were so caked with snow that it looked like Fred Flintstone's car and it drove like it, too!. But, Praise the Lord, we arrived safe and sound, and just in time for the Super Bowl! There was a party and a chili cook-off at the Eagles Club. It was like a celebration just for us. I was so glad to be back in Skagway with my new man!!

Will and I lived together for two years. After all the ups and downs we had both encountered, we wanted to be sure we were well suited to each other. Then the Lord laid it on our hearts and we began to talk about marriage.

Neither of us had been married before or had any kids, so it was a clean slate for both of us. I had dreamed of a proposal up on the gold mining claim. I'm just a romantic at heart!

We spent Thanksgiving in Atlin. It snowed and snowed and snowed. Will had fifteen thousand dollars worth of gold that one of his miner friends wanted him to sell. Looking at the gleaming masses was bringing out the madam in me, and I started getting mischievous ideas. I looked at Will with a naughty smile and batted my eyes at him. I nodded at the gold. "Wouldn't it be a great story for the madam and the miner??"

I've never read a Harlequin Romance with an interlude on a pile of gold, so we just had to make it up as we went along. It was incredibly erotic! Waking up was a little less so. The mattress was cold, and soaking wet. The snow had melted on the roof of our cozy little love nest, run down through the electrical socket and dripped all over the bed.

"Will, GET UP! The bed is SOAKING WET!"

Everything was so wet; we had to move into the living room. We dragged a twin mattress in from the spare room and grabbed a blanket off the couch. As we snuggled up and tried to keep warm, Will leaned over and said, "I'm not on my knees, but if we can live through the tough times, we can live through the happy times. Will you marry me?"

My heart was singing with joy. I snuggled closer and cried, "YES, YES, YES!!"

I was flying high all the way through until Christmas. Christmas in Skagway is kind of a fun time. All the tourists and summer residents are gone, and all that's left behind are tough-as-nails locals. It's pretty quiet throughout the fall and winter, but on Christmas Eve, we all get together at the Eagles Club for the annual party. Santa and his elves come to visit and hand out gifts to the kids. The church choir sings and there are lots of skits and entertainment.

We also hold the drawing for the American Legion Christmas Doll, which has been held for over 50 years. Every year the doll gets a replica of a wedding gown of a local lady, plus 6 outfits are sewn by local women. The dresses are spectacular, custom made by Jean Worley, who is a local Customs and Border Protection Officer. I have always thought she deserves the "Woman of the Year" award for all she does for the community, along with her husband Boyd, who is Port Director. Both are wonderful people!

I was excited because I was giving the doll away that Christmas. I was ready to go up on stage with my sister, who was to pick the winning number. But Will switched places with her and came up on stage. I was really surprised, as he is a very shy guy. He really blew my socks off when he took the microphone, got down on his hands and knees and said, "Cindy, I want to ask you to marry me in front of the whole town of Skagway. Will you marry me??" He took out a *huge* pink sapphire ring. I had been eyeing that ring for months. It's bright fuchsia and looks like something Zsa Zsa Gabor would be proud to wear. Bling for a miner's wife!!

I was speechless. I was shocked. I even got shy, and I'm not a shy kinda gal.

Tears rolling down my face, I screamed, "YES!" I was the happiest girl on earth.

A few days later I stopped by The Skagway News Depot to chat with my friend, Denise, who manages the place. The owner Jeff was also there. He grinned at me and said, "Guess who made the front page of the paper?"

Lo and behold, it was me and Will. Never in a million years did I think Will Godbey had it in him to propose on stage in front of the whole town. That's my miner!!

We had planned to get married at Will's gold mine, but unfortunately, the road washed away four days before the wedding. What to do? We were blessed with good friends who offered us their gold mine at the last minute. Daniel moved in two D9 bulldozers. Overnight, Gale and her friend Angelica did the place up like a movie set. There was a red carpet leading up between the dozers to a beautiful willow arch beside Surprise Lake. Old boots with flowers planted in them gave added flair. Other friends lent their talents to make our day special. Scott played the accordion and Carol sang, "How Strong is My Love". The skies were clear and the sun was shining brightly. It was perfect.

My brother Bill walked me down the aisle in my custom made dress. For my big day, Jean Worley, my best friend and seamstress of 17 years, made me a beautiful wedding dress in the style of 1898 in a cream color and gold lame. Jean also made me a stunning hat of gold satin trimmed in gold roses and purple ribbons. Our local corset maker Cory Giacomazzi made me a gorgeous fitted gold satin corset. Rita Prothero and Jan Tronrud brought boas in honor of celebrating our "The Madam and the Miner" wedding. Rita and Jan wore the purple and white ostrich feather boas and presented them to me to top off my beautiful dress for pictures. I was bursting with happiness as I walked towards my miner and my future! Who would've thought that all those years of going wherever the wind took me were leading to this!!

Before heading to the reception to celebrate, we had just one thing to do. We hopped in a helicopter and went out to our gold mine. We picnicked on the white sandy beach, just the two of us. It was the start of our life together and we enjoyed having a quiet moment to relish our newlywed status.

After our picnic, the helicopter came back to pick us up and deliver us to the reception. It was time to party!!

The reception was held in the nearby town of Atlin, on a

boat called the Tarahne. In the gold rush days, there was no road into Atlin, and prospectors had to travel up the lake by boat. In the roaring twenties, the Tarahne carried wealthy tourists who had come to enjoy the spectacular scenery and wacky outings such as midnight champagne cruises to see the glacier.

Today, the Tarahne is dry docked right on the lake in front of town, and looks much the same as it did 100 years ago. The historical setting was ideal for the Madam and the Miner. Friends had decorated for us and the whole boat was filled with flowers and twinkling lights. While Heather had been doing flowers, Lorna had set up the wedding cake she had made. It was a three tiered cake with a fountain made of miniature gold pans, complete with "nuggets" and tiny madam and miner kewpie dolls on top that looked just like me and Will. They were even dressed like us! Irises and yellow roses added the finishing touch.

There was a gal dressed in a roaring twenties costume playing ragtime tunes on a piano and Dave, a fellow entertainer from Liarsville, did magic tricks for the kids. With the fabulous food provided by Trudy and Tracy, it was a fun day for everyone.

We made it a weekend celebration in true northern style. We rented cabins on the lake, barbequed moose, elk, caribou and bear meat, and just enjoyed being together. Having our loved ones close made our wedding weekend an unforgettable experience. What more could a girl ask for? But there was more to come!

We set out for our honeymoon and did it up in style. We took our camper to the lower 48 to visit family and friends and finished up at Disney World before heading across the pond to check out Scotland and England. We were gone for two and a half months. Now *that's* what I call a honeymoon!!

***

Will & Cindy Godbey The Miner & the Madam Together At Last!

Bridal Picnic on the shore of Beautiful Suprise Lake on Cracker Creek

Gold Nuggets, Yellow Roses & Irises
Cutting the Cake at Reception aboard the
historic Tarahne, Atlin, BC

"The Tarahne" Sailed Atlin Lake from 1917 to 1936

UP THE CREEK

The winters in Alaska are long and cold. Sometimes it can get a person feeling a bit down, but now and again I think that we need some quiet time to recharge from the busy summer season and reminisce about all the good times we have had. On winter evenings, I often drift away, back to my days of gold mining on our claim on Cracker Creek.

Cracker Creek is at the end of Surprise Lake, near Atlin, British Columbia. Atlin is only sixty miles over the mountains from Skagway, but to drive there takes about three hours. Atlin has its own little place in Gold Rush history. The Gold Rush of 1898 centers around Dawson City, and the incredibly difficult journey and hardships that went along with it. In 1899, there was a gold strike in the Atlin area, which precipitated a smaller rush. The White Pass Yukon Railway was under construction at the time, and many of the men working on the railway jumped off and headed to the Discovery Gold Rush in Atlin, sometimes "borrowing" the shovels and picks they were using to start their grubstake. It is rumored that all the shovels in town went missing (5,000 from the Railroad alone) when the Atlin Gold Rush began.

Today, there is little left that hints at the huge numbers of gold seekers that poured into the area. Instead, there is the sleepy little town of Atlin, situated on Atlin Lake, the largest natural lake in British Columbia. Surrounded by mountains and forests, Atlin has often been referred to as "The Little Switzerland of the North". There is a friendly and peaceful quality about Atlin. Everyone knows everyone else and what they're doing, and if they don't, they just make something up!

In 2001, I was recovering from surgery, but there had been some complications and I was unable to sing or perform. My husband Will, and his friend Bill Campbell were planning on mining the Cracker Creek claim, and Will said, "Why don't you take the summer off and come mining with me?"

Faced with the choice of staying home by myself, or mining with my husband, I decided to go for it. Although when it was all over, I would never again think of it as "taking the summer off." Mining can be a lot of work!

In my shows, I always tell people about the Madams mining the miners, gold diggers extraordinaire! I decided it was time to try my hand at gold digging. So we set out, hand in hand, the Gold Miner and the Gold Digger, to see what we could find. Gold mining is a gamble at the best of times, but my husband has a Masters Degree in Geophysics Engineering, so he knows the lay of the land and where to look for the gold. I prayed for the Lord to tell me where to dig, and Will said it looked like the most likely place to strike it rich.

Cracker Creek starts at an elevation of 3000 feet at Surprise Lake and goes up to a glacial cirque at about 5,500 feet with mountains of nearly 7000 feet all around it. The snow isn't all gone until mid-June and then it comes back again in the beginning October. That leaves a pretty short mining season. You have to work fast and have a plan. First thing, Will built a road and we set up a camp.

We decided to put the camp down by Surprise Lake so we could sleep away from all the dust and bugs that we stirred up while mining. The incredible view was quite a perk and sort of made up for the drawbacks of living in a makeshift camp. And makeshift it was. For some strange reason, the water didn't want to run uphill through the hose to our shower. Sometimes it was more of a dribble than a shower.

Being the miner's wife, I was the obvious choice for camp cook, but I told the men, "If you want me to cook, I want a tent to cook in. You can get one from Wal-Mart."

They complained a bit about that, they didn't want to spend the fifty bucks for a screened in tent, but I insisted. So, I got the tent. Praise the Lord! The mosquitoes and black flies were so horrendous at times that you couldn't see the face of the person you were talking to. Of course, there were only three of us in a seven-mile radius, and I guess they have to eat too. We were probably a nice change from the critters they were used to.

That tent kept the rain off and we could eat and rest in peace while enjoying the view. It was the best investment we made that season. For all their complaining about having to buy it, I think those guys spent more time in that tent than they did up the creek. Some days I had to chase them out into the weather and the bugs so they could get some work done. No wonder some of the miners during the Gold Rush went a little crazy.

At night, Bill slept in his car, and Will and I slept in Will's greasy, grimy old mining van. It was full of tools, and there was a dirty smelly old mattress. Before I went to sleep, I would wrestle all the tools out from under my head and my feet. But it kept the bugs away, and when it got cold, we could turn the heat on. I was mighty grateful for that. That van was a blessing from God and I was thankful. It was also protection from the bears.

I am deathly afraid of bears. When I was a kid, a bear tried to get into our car, but thank God, we got away. A dear friend of mine was actually killed by a bear, poor girl. All my bear experiences made me bear aware. Obsessed actually.

I always carried around a spray bottle of ammonia solution. I sprayed it on the tires of the van, and my shoes and walking up to the mine. I learned that trick from an Atlin miner. He told me that bears don't like smells that burn their nose. One time a black bear was charging at him, and he dumped the ammonia solution on a rock and threw it at the bear. All it took was one smell and that bear high tailed it out of there.

But, mining isn't all glamour. I have never worked so hard in my life. Most days, we worked eighteen hours. We all got in better shape, because we were always doing something. When I got back into town, people said, " Man! You look good! Whatchya been doing, some kind of weight loss program?"

"Hardly," I told them. "Just mining."

Walking the mile between camp and the mine was a workout in itself. We had to wear mosquito netting, I wore bug pants and top to keep the little buggers out of my clothes. Maybe they were just upset because we were destroying their houses with our digging. Punishing the home wreckers, I guess!

The weather wasn't always the greatest either. It can get cold up at that elevation, and we had our fair share of rain and wind. It was just like a woman. You never knew what to expect and the temperature was always changing.

Lum, one of the local miners from Ruby Creek, gave Will and me a very small little trailer. It was 12' x 6' and it was oval. It looked like an egg. We put it up at the mine so I would have a place to prepare lunch and snacks for the guys. It had a little table that sat four people, a small stove and sink, and a little bunk bed above the table. We never used the bed though, we were afraid it would break. I loved that little trailer; it was so cute. I learned to draw and paint in there, and cooked up some mighty fine meals, too.

Since we were right in the middle of a bunch of dirt, I decided to make a fun and colorful garden outside. I got a bunch of gold paint and spray painted all the big boulders and planted fake flowers everywhere. It was a summer haven. It was funny to watch the bees and butterflies come by and land on the flowers, though sometimes I felt bad that there was no honey for them.

There were lots of interesting things to see around that mine. As we were setting up earlier that year, we had noticed an old mining tunnel from times past. We looked up the mining records and discovered that they had actually found some gold there. There was an old cabin nearby that looked like it may have housed a blacksmith at one time and a few other cabins with doghouses scattered about. The miners had dog teams and used them to pull and move the huge boulders so they could dig their tunnels. You can still see the entrance into the tunnels, but they have caved in and are no longer safe.

Thank God we had heavy equipment to do a lot of the work. It's still hard, but not nearly as hard as it would have been in the old days.

Bill ran the loader and Will was on the backhoe. They were moving dirt through the sluice box. My job was to move the big rocks with a shovel and a crowbar, and wash away the dirt with a hose. I was also the cook, preparing three meals a day and snacks. Sort of seems like I had the toughest job of all. Hmmmm.

Yup, I was one cookin' babe. Sometimes it smelled so good, the guys would follow their noses right into the trailer for some home baked goodies before they even knew what they were doing. It's true, the way to get a man to do anything, really, is to appeal to his appetite. In the old days, camp cooks were treated very carefully; their word was law. You didn't mess with the cook. Something I'll have to keep in mind in case I ever take another "summer off" to work at a gold mine. HA!

For all the hard work and obstacles, there were just as many benefits. Living in the mountains by a lake with sandy beaches isn't a bad way to spend the summer. The fishing was fantastic; we ate a lot of fresh grayling. After work, we would relax by the water or lay under the stars, looking for constellations or counting shooting stars.

We had company out there too. Moose, black bears, grizzly bears, caribou, eagles and beavers - nature's little engineers, busy, busy, making dams everywhere. If you had good eyesight, you could even see the mountain goats grazing way up on the highest hills.

One day, Will and I explored some of the old cabins. It was a fascinating look back in time at all the hardships and courage those miners had. There were a lot of rusty old cans around, mostly beans. Add that to a steady diet of rice, fish and wild game, they were regular gourmets!

As we were poking around, we noticed some fresh moose tracks, with some baby moose tracks alongside. We got out of there fast, hollering all the way back down to camp in order to scare her off if she still happened to be nearby. A cow moose with a calf is a very dangerous. She will charge and stomp you flatter than a pancake to protect her baby. We lived around many wild animals. You have to be aware of their presence and respect them. It's really important to keep your campsite clean so there is nothing to tempt them or make them curious. By doing that, you encourage them to stay away from people and hopefully avoid dangerous encounters.

Of course, if you are out in the bush long enough, close encounters are inevitable. One cool autumn day, Will was moving the loader further up the creek, and I was to follow him in the truck to bring him back. It was a rough and rugged road, and I was just meandering along and singing away to my praise music, thanking the Lord for His beautiful creation. There wasn't another soul for miles and I didn't have a care in the world.

I came upon a clearing right before crossing a creek, when out of nowhere came an enormous bull caribou with a rack that would've landed him in the record books. He was running full speed ahead and coming right towards me. It jolted me back to reality, my heart pounding. We both came to a screeching halt, and eyed each other warily, neither one of us had been expecting company.

Steam flowed out of his nostrils and floated off into the chilly air as he panted and snorted. He had been running hard, as if he was being chased by a bear, or maybe he was doing the chasing and there was a little lady caribou somewhere nearby.

Our eyes met and time stopped. I could feel the power flowing from this magnificent animal. Then he turned away and headed into the bush. I sat for a moment, weak with the realization that he had literally almost ran over me. It was a moment I will never forget. I wonder if he felt the same? One never knows!

Will and Bill Boyko, another one of Will's old partners, had an encounter of their own that was a little more unsettling several years before this adventure of mine. They had finished prospecting for the day and they hopped into the Argo, which is sort of like a little bumper car on tracks. They are great for all kinds of terrain, and they even float.

The guys were tired and ready for a shower and a hot meal. They were cruising home at top speed; about 20mph. Climbing uphill out of the creek bed slowed them down to about 10mph, the perfect time to look through the clearing and spot a big ole grizzly bear about a quarter mile away.

Will gunned it, but as he gained speed, the grizzly started sprinting through the forest. It turned into a game of hide and seek. After the fourth burst of speed, he disappeared from sight. Bill and Will came into a stand of trees. That big grizzly jumped out of the trees right into the middle of the road and turned and looked straight at the guys. SURPRISE!!

Then he stood up on his hind legs and started growling and yowling at Will and Bill. "GET OFF MY ROAD!!"

Will decided that would be a good time to get out his shotgun and take aim. He had that gun on the grizzly for a good twenty minutes. Heart pounding, Will said, "You come any closer, you're dead!"

The bear was still jumping up and down, growling and screaming, but there was nowhere else for them to go, so they sat and waited it out for half an hour. Will was ready to shoot, but finally, the bear backed down and left. But not before he stuck out his tongue and spit on the ground. Horrible manners.

What an *animal*. The guys came back to camp, bragging about how that bear barely got out alive. I bet that bear was swaggering around the woods and saying the same thing about them!!

Now back to my gold mining story...we stayed and mined until we got snowed out. We found about two hundred dollars worth of gold, not enough to even cover our groceries for the summer. But, I always tell people that it's not about the gold. It's about witnessing and enjoying God's creation. We had fresh fish everyday, a warm place to sleep, good food to eat, great friendship and lots of laughs. We worked hard, and in our own way, we relived the gold rush from a century past. We had God's blessings. The gold is His and if He wants us to find it, He'll show us where it is. In the meantime, I know He'll bless us with many more golden moments up on Cracker Creek.

"Grub's Ready, Come & Get It!"

Will & Big Nugget

Finding Gold

A Woman's Work Is Never Done!

Dolly and Eagle Chicks

Daniel Johnson, Dolly & Tutshi

MY "LOVE AFFAIR"
WITH ROBIN WILLIAMS

Movie stars? In *Skagway?* You bet! Alaska is a magical place, and if you stay here long enough, you will see things that you probably wouldn't see anywhere else!

A few years, back a bunch of folks from Hollywood came to Skagway to film a movie. Giovanni Ribisi, Woody Harrelson, Holly Hunter, Alison Lohman, and, you guessed it, Robin Williams!

The movie is a dark comedy called "The Big White". Holly Hunter's character is a woman with Tourettes Syndrome. She swears *a lot*. I didn't know that Tourettes is a real disorder until I watched the movie. But there were some funny parts too, I liked it better the second time I watched it. I think I was too busy looking for cameos by Skagway locals to really pay attention to the story line the first time!

Robin Williams, Holly Hunter, Giovanni, Allison, the directors and the producers all stayed at the Mile Zero B&B and the Whitehouse B&B. The owners of both B&B's are good friends of mine. I stop at the Mile Zero often to have tea with owner, Tara, and her mom, Judy. Sometimes we have girls' night and watch movies or just hang out and visit. But when the stars came to town, *nobody* was allowed to visit.

I walk every day, and of course I would deliberately walk past the Mile Zero, cool as a cucumber, like I wasn't even paying attention to a house full of *movie stars*. Then, when no one was looking, I would do a quick glance over the house, just in case I might see Robin Williams running around in his underwear. All I needed was one quick look. In my mind, I could even see the color of the underwear. No luck, so I would keep walking straight ahead, then sneak another quick look to see if I could see who was in which room.

I was on secret movie star watch. I didn't think anyone knew what I was up to, and they probably didn't, most likely they were all too busy doing the same thing to even notice. After the stars all left town, we all talked about the "star watching" and had a good laugh about it.

The stars were all over town, walking, bicycling, hiking the trails, buying dinners and hanging out with the locals. They were making their movie up on the Klondike Highway. They were in town for the whole month of April. Tourist season hadn't started yet, so we had them to ourselves. After a long, cold, boring winter, it was thrilling to have Hollywood movie stars buzzing around Skagway.

Everyone I talked to was meeting Robin Williams and Holly Hunter, but I wasn't having any luck. I started asking Jesus every night in my prayers to let me meet them, but still, nothing. So I said, "OK Lord, you pick the time and place."

That night, I went to Broadway video and rented every Robin Williams movie they had, plus "The Piano" with Holly Hunter. The "three of us" had a pajama party with nachos, popcorn and root beer floats. I stayed up all night watching movies and dreaming of meeting Robin Williams in person.

The next day was the Easter Sunrise Service at Pullen Pond. Pullen Pond is up against the mountainside, over by the railroad dock. It's a grassy park with a BBQ and picnic area and a few trees, so you can picnic in the shade. In August, the salmon spawn there.

The Easter Sunrise Service begins at 7:30 A.M. on Easter Sunday and the preachers from all five churches take part. We pray, we sing and just drink in the crisp morning air. The sky is streaked with pink from the morning sunshine. I love it and try to go every year.

At the end of the service, I saw a few of my girlfriends over on the other side of the pond. I started waving and yelling, "Hello, Hello, HELLO!" There was a man about six feet in front of me; he was wearing a hat and a nice dress coat. When I started yelling, he turned around and looked at me.

I said, "I'm not talking to you, buddy, I'm trying to get my girlfriends' attention."

Then I realized who he was. It gave me a jolt. "AAAAAH!" I screamed really loud. He jumped, and then he screamed back at me. It was definitely a Robin Williams moment. I had been thinking I would never meet him, and now that I finally had, I was completely unprepared. I stood there, looking at the ground and started swaying back and forth. In my best "Rain Man" imitation, I just stood there, staring at the ground, saying, "Welcome to Skagway. Welcome to Skagway. Welcome to Skagway."

I never imagined I would meet Robin Williams at church, but God had a plan. SURPRISE!! I guess it goes to show that God just laughs when we make our own plans, and I bet he had a chuckle that day. But He had more laughs in store.

The Haven restaurant is a great place to eat, as the stars had discovered. Holly Hunter would wave to me like we were old pals, and I actually hung out with her make up artist for a few hours one day and got some great makeup tips. For instance, did you know that if you put blush on your cleavage, you will look more perky and voluptuous? Who knew! It's great when Hollywood comes to you- I use that little trick all the time! (I was only a DDD --- at the time!) Try it sometime!

Anyways, back to the Haven. Sometimes when I am out on my daily walks, I stop in there for a bathroom break. Their restrooms are so spacious; it's my favorite place for a pit stop if I don't think I can make it home. Well, on this particular day, I was in a rush to get there, as it was rather urgent. There happened to be a man standing by the open door, talking to the chef. In my hurry to get past him, I tripped and fell right into his arms. And there I was, face-to-face and nose-to-nose with Robin Williams. Praise the Lord; I had just had a breath mint.

We stood there clutching each other tightly; afraid to let

go for fear that we would both fall down in a big heap. He was looking into my eyes and I'm sure we looked like we belonged in "Gone With the Wind". I said, oh-so-calmly, "Hello, Robin."

He smiled an adorable smile and said in a sexy voice that sent chills up my spine, "Oh! It's *you* again!" I could have stood there, locked in his arms forever, if alarm bells hadn't started going off in my bladder. But I had to go. Literally.

So, one last adoring look, and I fluttered off down the hall with a smile that would last a month, and an idea that God was having another giggle at my "love affair" with Robin Williams!

✳✳✳

Dawson Dolly & Robin Williams
Art Work by Stacy Eaton

DOG SLEDDING AND PUPPY BREATH

On Thanksgiving weekend, my husband Will and I ran away to celebrate life and count our many blessings. On Thanksgiving Day we had a wonderful dinner with some old friends who are gold miners. We had lots of laughs and talked about leasing out our hard rock gold mining claims to some big investors.

The next day we headed out to Muktuk Ranch to stay in a cabin on the river and go dog sledding. The road to the ranch wound down and around and around. Just as I was beginning to think we would never arrive, there we were. 100 excited husky dogs were there to greet us. What a racket! We checked into our cabin and were told what time we were scheduled to go mushing the next day.

The rustic little cabin had two bedrooms and a small kitchen and living room. There was no running water and no electricity, but thank goodness, it had an outhouse and a honey bucket. Praise the Lord for the small things in life!

The window was broken and needed changing and the camp help needed to bring us some water and start the woodstove to warm the place up, so we decided to head to the hot springs for a soak while they got everything ready.

The hot springs were so relaxing and we actually met some new friends in the pool! It was a cold winter night and the northern lights were dancing about the sky in purples, greens and reds. You could hear them crackling as they danced. We whistled and they moved down closer to us. There is just nothing like soaking in a hot pool watching the northern lights.

When we arrived back at the cabin, the window was fixed and the fire was burning. Warm and cozy, it looked right out onto the river, peaceful and serene. But, the long drive had been tiring and the hot springs had made us drowsy, so we turned in for the night. Will was snoring away but I was too excited about dog sledding to go right to sleep.

I slipped back in time a few years, to my 50th birthday. My girlfriend, Susan, had surprised me and whisked me away in a helicopter, up to the glacier to go dog sledding. I was very excited, but also very nervous. I was not sure what I was getting into. Our guide was a musher from France, named Jacque. He drove first then Susan took a turn. I was last. I was so nervous and wasn't sure if I could drive or not. But, I hopped on the back of the sled and away we went. It was white out conditions and somewhat of a blizzard, so it was really hard to see.

The dogs were pretty happy and energetic because they knew they were headed back to camp, so we just flew like the wind. I was standing on the back of the sled trying to keep my feet straight and work the brake pad. It is constant foot work when you are flying down the trail, trying to control the dogs and just hang on. I was dressed in a heavy parka and my seventy below bunny boots. I had silver fox mittens and a beaver hat. I looked like the Pillsbury Dough Boy's dream date - but I was warm!

I remember hanging on for dear life and my hands and face were numb with fear. We were flying over big ice moguls, one after another. I was sure I was going to fly off and slide down the glacier into a crevasse and never be seen again. It was not a smooth ride and I was terrified. I swore I would never EVER go dog sledding again.

And here I was preparing for another dog sledding adventure. Still unable to sleep, I found my husband's head lamp and started looking at the books in the cabin, hoping to find some tips. I was in luck. I came across "Beginners Dog Mushing." I find it a fascinating sport and, as I read, I began to feel more comfortable about the whole thing.

After all, the whole reason for this trip was to help me get over my awful experience on the glacier. I read for awhile longer and finally managed to sleep.

Morning came and the sun shone through the window. There were a few small coals from the fire left in the woodstove, but we could see our breath, so Will got the fire going and warmed the place up again. Then he made bacon and eggs, the perfect breakfast for a cold winters day.

I started reading my Bible and praying that my anxiety would go away. I almost cancelled, but I was bound and determined to get over my fear. Will had planned on going with us, but at one time he had actually done a three year stint as a musher. I guess some of the glamor of the whole thing was now lost for him, he decided to stay behind and relax. So, I made lunch and then headed out on my adventure.

I arrived at the Lodge and was again greeted by the dogs. 100 barking huskies of all shapes and colors. They were all racing dogs and they were champing at the bit to get going! The owner of the place, Frank, is a long time musher and has raced 24 times in the "Yukon Quest", a famous Canadian dog sled race. He told me not to be nervous, as the dogs will sense it, just flow with the sled and have fun with it!

I thought, "OK, change the thought and change the experience, I will have no fear and I'll have a ball!" Yeah, right. Easier said than done.

My designated dog sledding partner was a gal named Leese. She was a real sweetheart and had a very calming and gentle personality. She was also a skilled musher. She got me outfitted and ready to go. It can get very cold on the trail with the wind blowing in your face, so you need to dress warmly. I wore my rabbit hat and insulated coveralls, a red down coat and silver fox mittens.

Leese gave me a crash course on how to ride the sled. Then we went to meet the six dogs who would be taking us on our journey. I petted and talked to all of them and asked them to PLEASE be nice to me. Leese showed me how to harness them up, so I was part of the team and did my duty.

The two lead dogs were Belle and Zinc, followed by Inch, Vanek, Marley and Cola. I asked Leese to drive first, so I jumped in the basket and down the trail we went.

The dogs are bred for the sport and they love to go sledding. Their spirits were high and they were excited. The weather was perfect. The temperature was zero and the sun was shining brightly. It had snowed the night before and the trees were glittering white. It was truly a winter wonderland.

"MUSH!" hollered Leese from the back of the sled. I was tucked into the basket with a red canvas wrapped over top of me, snug as a bug. "Good dogs!" Leese called lovingly to the dogs.

As we were headed out of the woods, the icicles were breaking off of the trees and falling into my lap. I was still pretty nervous and my mouth was dry, but they worked wonders to quench my thirst. We arrived at the Takhini River and headed down through the canyon. Sledding on a frozen river can be a bit scary but I was assured that it was frozen *solid*. My view from the basket was six furry little dog rear ends. Thank God we stopped for them to do their business. If they do it on the run, you can end up with it flying right at you. It's all part of the fun!

The dogs were cruising at about 10 miles per hour, a nice and easy pace. I could feel the sunshine and the wind on my face. The canyon, the forest and river were absolutely beautiful. It was so quiet, the only sounds were the dogs' feet on the snow and crackle of the sled flying over the ice of the river.

When we went around corners, I had to lean towards the turn. Leese would holler "Gee!" when she wanted them to turn right and "Ha" to turn left, "Whoa" to stop. Parts of the river were a bit rough, but nothing like I experienced on the glacier. Most of the trail was smooth sailin'. Chunks of ice were stacked up off to the sides. Thankfully, Frank had groomed the trail with his snow machine to flatten out the rough spots. We didn't tip the sled over once, which was just as well , some of those ice chunks can be pretty sharp.

Our excursion was to last about two hours, so we stopped often and let the dogs rest. Then we came to an island in the river. We were half way. And it was my turn to drive.

By now, the dogs had burned some of that energy off. Tongues hanging out, they were rolling in the snow to cool off and eating a bit to get a drink. I was feeling a bit thirsty myself, and thought it was a good idea, so I grabbed a handful. Leese hollered, "Don't eat the yellow snow!"

I hadn't been paying attention, but luckily she was. I said, "Thanks for saving me, Leese!" and we both laughed. It helped ease the tension of knowing that I was about to take over the driving. Leese got into the basket and I hopped on the back of the sled.

"MUSH!" I said, and the dogs started cruising. We were off.

Tipping the sled over on corners happens a lot when mushing, so after I managed the first few with no mishaps, I started to relax a bit and breathe easier. I had been hyperventilating earlier and now my oxygen deprived brain was starting to get back to normal as I swayed with the movement of the sled.

The trail seemed to be getting better and smoother and my fear started to diminish. I could feel the temperature drop as the wind picked up and the sun went down. The dogs were happy and picked up their pace once they knew we were heading back home.

By now, I was feeling pretty confident. I had to do the fancy foot work to keep us from going off course, but the trail on the river was so much smoother than being on the glacier and flying over big moguls. I was actually enjoying myself! Once we got closer to home, I asked Leese to take over. I jumped back into the basket and wrapped up in the red tarp. As we wound our way through the forest, we brushed against the trees and they dropped fresh snow all over me. My legs were cramped in the basket and a bit stiff from maneuvering the sled, but I had a smile of pure joy on my face. I was so proud of myself for overcoming my fear. As I sat in the basket, I realized how much I had enjoyed the afternoon. Driving the dogs was fun, but I really liked being the passenger and looking at the scenery.

When we arrived back at home, all the other dogs started barking, welcoming us home. If felt good to be loved. And it felt *really* good to have arrived safe and sound. I hugged Leese and thanked her. Her support and kindness had made the whole thing fun for me.

A perfect finish to the day was when Edward took me to play with the puppies. They were so cute and fuzzy and cuddly. The smell of puppy breath after dog mushing through pristine wilderness. Can't beat that!

Dog Mushing on Harding Glacier, Skagway, AK

Another Handsome Admirer

Puppy Love

DOLLY AND POLAR BEARS ON TOP OF THE WORLD

I love being an entertainer. It is such a unique way to connect with people and I never get tired of it. In my time as Madam Dolly, I have done walking tours, brothel tours, bus tours, train rides, you name it. I feel truly blessed to be one of the fortunate few who really fits in her job and loves it. I did tours at the Klondike Gold Dredge in Skagway for seven years and during that time, I was honored with the Princess Cruise Line Tour Guide of the Year Award, three years in a row. You just couldn't find a better job!

And you just never know where it's going to take you. I seek guidance from the Lord on the direction my life is going and really try to listen when He speaks to me. On the last day of my last season at the Dredge, I woke up to God telling me I had to go to the Top of the World. Barrow, Alaska.

"No, Lord," I said, "You mean, you need me to go to Mexico!"

Nope. Barrow, Alaska.

"Lord, wherever you tell me to go, I will go, but just *know* you have the wrong person, as it's almost October and it's *cold and dark* in Barrow. So, I'll pray about this all day, and then at bedtime, we shall see where you really want me to go."

I prayed on it all day long. That evening, just for kicks and giggles, I checked out airfare to Barrow. It was actually quite cheap. So, I figured what the heck? I called around to some hotels. I got the last room available in town. Then I called the airline. I got the last seat on the plane. And I was goin' to BARROW, ALASKA!!

Had I gone mad? Some people thought so. So much for my fun in the sun in Mexico. My pastor Ray, and his wonderful wife Cheri had always wanted to go to Barrow, so I thought they would be the perfect companions. Unfortunately, also being our chief of police keeps Ray pretty busy and they were unable to go. So I invited Pat, an old friend of mine. We were so excited about our adventure and geared up to have FUN! All the arrangements fell into place.

The first person we met on the plane was a lovely gal named Lula Falleaf. She is also a believer and we just hit it right off. She has a beautiful voice and has recorded some wonderful praise music. I bought a few of her CD's while we were still in the air.

All we could see was the frozen tundra and the Arctic Ocean. It looked like a whole different world. When we arrived, we went off to find our lodging. Barrow Bed and Breakfast was a beautiful place. There was a big open kitchen looking into a large living room. There was a bed in the living room as well as another bedroom and a big bathroom with a sink for each of us. Home sweet home! The best place in town and really nice hosts to boot. The Lord really takes care of us!

Pat and I had booked an eight-hour tour with Arctic Adventures, so off we went. Our tour guide was wonderful. He was an Inupiaq Inuit named Sam Leavitt. He was fifty-five years old and he was pretty new to guiding. It was a real bonus, because he was interested and excited about his job, and it showed. He really wanted to show us a good time.

He showed us all around town and introduced us to local carvers, all the while regaling us with stories and interesting bits of information. Pat and I were the only ones on the tour, so we had his undivided attention. We laughed a lot and shared some really special moments.

Through Sam, we learned that Barrow has about 4,500 residents and probably the harshest weather in Alaska. It is one of the largest Inupiat Inuit settlements where traditional culture and modern life have blended together. Fishing, hunting and whaling are just a way of life. The North Slope oil discovery has brought wealth to the area, including modern influences such as snowmobiles, but it has been continuously occupied for 5,000 years by people who have learned to live in the climate. That's a long time to live in the cold!

Sam told us that the Land of the Midnight Sun is especially true in Barrow. The sun shines and never sets for 82 days in the summer, from early May to early August. Then it's dark for 51 to 67 days in the winter. On clear nights it's a good time to view the northern lights and go dog sledding. Spring whaling occurs in May. The whalers go out into the ocean in 16-foot seal skin boats. Their wives spend long hours sewing the skins of bearded seals to put around the outside of the boat. They all pray before they go out, and during the hunt.

The men watch and wait in the whaling houses until they see the first sign of a bowhead whale emerging. Then five men jump into a boat and quietly approach the whale. When it surfaces, they use harpoons. Once the kill is made, they use ropes to drag the whale to shore and up onto land. When they return, they give thanks for a successful hunt that ensures food supplies for the winter.

Once Sam had showed us all around Barrow, we stopped for mochas and goodies, then headed out towards the point. The point is a spit of land that runs out into the Arctic Ocean, just north of town. To the left is the Chukchi Sea and to the right is the Beaufort Sea. Both seas run together and form the Arctic Ocean. It's a very unique landscape, like no other on earth. It looks like another planet.

We were on a mission, looking for polar bears. We cruised around the black sand dunes in Sam's big old truck. We saw lots of birds and some white arctic foxes taking refuge from the wind under a rusty old barrel. It was late in the afternoon when we finally made it to the northern-most point of North America. We stood on the farthest shore North looking at the Arctic Ocean and trying to absorb all the information Sam had given us. Praise the Lord! I was standing on the Top of the

World, munching on a salmon sandwich!! Unbelievable!!
It was late afternoon. It had already been a full day. We had
seen all the sights, taken lots of pictures and had lots of
laughs. Bouncing around in the truck as we traveled down
the rough road on the way back to town, we were feeling
pretty weary. My attention wandered as I gazed across the
tundra.

Suddenly I yelled, "POLAR BEAR OVER THERE!!!"
Sam hit the gas and we sped down the beach so we could get
closer. He was a huge and powerful animal. Just magnificent!
We followed him closely and took pictures until he picked
up the pace and shot off down the beach. When the coast
was clear, we got out to look at his footprints. Pat put her
boot along side one of the prints. It was twice the size of her
foot.

By this time, the mocha had worked its way through my
system, but we were far from any facilities, so I crouched
down and peed in a polar bear track. That was definitely a
first for me!

Sam said that the bear was not fully grown and was probably
only four or five years old, but he sure looked BIG to Pat and
I. But, he was an amazing creature and we were thrilled at
seeing our first polar bear.

On our way home we stopped off at City Hall so we could
meet the Mayor. Michael Stotts was a really neat man with
such a kind heart. He said, "What brings you to Barrow?"
"The Lord sent me!!"

He smiled a great big smile and pointed to the wall at a copy
of the Ten Commandments. He said, "I'm a Christian, too!"
I was so happy to hear that. We chatted a bit longer and set
up a photo shoot for that Thursday so the Mayor could have
his picture taken with Dolly.

Thursday came and we arrived at the shoot. With Michael
was April, his secretary, and Tom, the Director of Assets
and Property. They were both real sweeties. Cindy Shults,

his official photographer, did the photographs, while Pat snapped a few photos from the side. We did the photo shoot under the famous ancient whaling arch on the Chukchi Sea. I was so excited!

After we finished, we all headed over to Pepe's Mexican Restaurant. That's right, Mexican food in the Arctic. It was the best I have ever had. The staff was great, so friendly. The owner, Fran Tate is a wonderful woman who is *always* smiling. She has owned Pepe's for thirty years. At eighty years of age, she still works seven days a week, probably why she looks so good, bless her heart! She reminded me of myself in some ways. She had some of that wild and crazy fun about her that comes from living in the north for a long time. I only hope that at eighty, I'm still going strong like Fran.

Back in 1984, someone did a write up on Fran in the Wall Street Journal. Someone read that article and sent it into Johnny Carson. Before you know it, Fran was off to appear on his show, not only for owning the northern-most Mexican restaurant in America, but also for being such an amazing and vibrant woman. For a gift, she presented Johnny with an oosik, which is a rather vital and private body part of a male walrus. Oddly enough, they just look like a long piece of ivory. Occasionally you will see one that has been intricately carved or made into a crib board. So, if you are ever traveling to the Top of the World, keep your eyes open and you might be lucky enough to bring back a souvenir that's a *real* conversation starter!

Fran has two sons, Mike and Joe. Joe is a very colorful character. He has actually turned his house into a museum! He has been collecting all kinds of ancient relics for many years that is so impressive that the Smithsonian has even been by to check it out and do some write ups about it.

I had told the Lord that I wanted to go to Mexico instead of Barrow, but he gave me a touch of Mexico in Pepe's. I had

such a great time there with Fran, it was better than Mexico.
God just laughs at the elaborate plans we humans make for
ourselves. His plans always work out better.

Just as we were finishing lunch, April got a call to tell her the
whalers had been successful and they were on their way in.
I was still dressed as Dolly, but there was no time to change.
We headed straight for the Point to await the arrival of the
victorious hunters.

There were four aluminum boats towing in the thirty-five
foot bowhead. They had it tied up with a rope and they were
trying to maneuver it through the ice buildup. When they got
close enough, they tied it to a backhoe and dragged it up on
shore.

It was very cold and windy that day, but it didn't dampen the
spirits. Everyone was so excited at the success of the hunt. It
was time to celebrate. Everyone had their picture taken with
the whale; the kids' were climbing all over it like it was a big
toy. CNN was even there doing some filming.

The captain Roy was Lula's brother. He took the first cut into
the whale and after that they used long blades to finish the job
and distribute portions to the towns' people. Once that's all
done, the bones and other remains are moved further down
the point for the bears, foxes and birds to clean up. Everyone
gets a share, and it keeps the polar bears out of town!

Oilskin tents were erected in Roy's front yard and the stoves
were set up. The whole town came, everyone bringing a
potluck dish and the celebration began. Everyone thanked
the captain for a successful hunt and for the food for the
winter.

We didn't make the party, but plates of food were delivered
right to our door with a few roasts to let us know we hadn't
been forgotten.

The Mayor had invited me to church for praise and worship.
Those people were just on *fire* for the Lord!! Then I headed
over to the Presbyterian Church. After giving my testimony

I met some really nice people. It was a blessing and an honor to worship with them.

The next morning, I met with Mike Shults from the city council. He is Fran's son and also the husband of Cindy, the photographer. He took me to the local radio station where I did a ten-minute interview. The station had been down all night and the signal came back on right as I started my interview. The first thing to hit the airwaves was the question, "What brought you to Barrow?"

"The Lord sent me!!"

"The Lord works in mysterious ways, doesn't he?" replied my interviewer.

The next day, Pat and Sam and I wanted to go and see more polar bears. Off we went. Within an hour, we saw five bears. We couldn't believe our luck! We sat eating salmon sandwiches while we watched a mama and her two cubs chewing on whale blubber only 100 feet away from us. It was surreal being that close. They are very dangerous animals, especially when they have their young nearby, but these were full and happily playing at tug-of-war with the blubber, then finally settling down to share.

Just then, we looked over to see a big male swimming towards us and the little family. As he got closer, the mama loved her cubs away and we moved too. Two weeks before we arrived, a man had been eaten by a polar bear in a nearby village while walking home one night. His pregnant wife got away, thank God, but it was a sad and horrible event.

As we cruised down the point to see some whalers testing their boats, I spotted another bear trying to lift his belly full of whale blubber onto an iceberg. He was so tired out from swimming. It took a few tries, but he finally made it and just collapsed from exhaustion. It was a magical day. Our new friend Sam was a wonderful guide, he really has the knack. Thank you Sam, you made our trip unforgettable!!

Pat and I were treated with such kindness and respect from all the townspeople. We made a lot of good friends in Barrow. I am so grateful I listened to the Lord and went to the Top of the World. Thank you Lord and Thank you Barrow!!

✳✳✳

Polar Bear Paw Prints!

"She's mine (growl) No, she's mine!"
Photo by Heather Mjolsness

"Forget it boys, I'm out of here."
Photo by Heather Mjolsness

Dawson Dolly with Mayor of Barrow, Alaska & Friends
Under the Famous Whaling Arch
Photo by Cindy Shults

SARAH PALIN MEETS DAWSON DOLLY

In my time as Dawson Dolly, I have had many unusual and exciting experiences and have been privileged to entertain thousands of people. And once in a blue moon, I even meet someone famous!

Sarah Palin was voted as one of "America's Top 10 Most Fascinating people of 2008" on a Barbara Walters ABC special. Most of you will remember her as the Nominee for Vice President when she ran with John McCain in the 2008 presidential elections.

Here in Alaska, we have known Sarah for much longer. Sarah Heath was born in Sandpoint, Idaho, but in 1964, her parents, Chuck and Sally, moved her and her three siblings to Skagway, Alaska. Chuck was a science teacher and track coach at the local high school. After five years in Skagway, they moved on to Wasilla. Sarah attended high school there, and in 1982, she was co-captain of the state championship basketball tournament.

In 1984, she won the Miss Wasilla pageant and went on to compete in the Miss Alaska contest where she finished as the third runner up. She graduated in 1987 with a BS in communications and journalism, and the following year, eloped to the Courthouse in Palmer with her high school sweetheart, Todd.

Sarah was destined for big things. She worked as a sportscaster for an Anchorage news station and in 1996, she was elected Mayor of Wasilla. She served two terms, totaling six years. She made history on December 4th 2006 when she was sworn in as the first woman and the youngest person ever to hold the office of Governor of Alaska. She is the "Most Popular Governor of Alaska" and I am grateful to have a governor that loves the Lord, as I do!

Sarah is a busy woman, with a lot on the go, but in the spring of 2008, the owners of the Chilkoot Trail OutPost Lodge, Kathy and Fred Hosford, invited Sarah and her family to come and stay. It was a perfect opportunity for Sarah to catch up with old friends from her childhood years in Skagway and meet some of the "new " people. (In the north, you aren't "officially" a local until you have lived somewhere for at least ten years.)

The party was held at the local Jewell Gardens. Charlotte and Jim, who own the gardens, have put many hours of hard work into creating a beautiful setting, and it was the perfect place for our Governor to meet the local people. Tons of flowers and delicious food! What more do you need for a great party? The whole town came out to socialize.

I had always admired Sarah for the many things she has done for the state of Alaska. I thought she seemed like a wonderful person and hoped to meet her one day.

The day of the "Meet & Greet" I was doing a show in a Parlor Car on the White Pass Train. I was all dressed up in my custom made red and gold 1898 dress and hat. (To look her best, a girl simply *must* have her own personal seamstress. Jean makes Dolly beautiful, bless her heart!)

I went straight from the show to the party, hoping I would at least get a glimpse of Sarah. God answered my prayers in a big way! It wasn't long before she looked my way and smiled her pretty sweet smile. "Who are you?" she asked warmly.

I was thrilled. I said, " I'm Dawson Dolly. I have the biggest nuggets in the Klondike! Would you like to hold my gold nugget?"

Her eyes opened wide. She said, " WOW! That's the biggest nugget I have ever seen!" She held the nugget and we had some pictures taken. Then she thanked me for making her day and said that I really had to go and find her dad so he could hold my nugget, too.

So, Chuck and Sally and I had our pictures taken together, and I got to chat with them for a bit. They were really sweet, fun people. I hear Chuck is still talking about Dolly's Gold Nugget!

It was a great experience to meet Sarah and her family, it's a day I will never forget! She has a heart of gold and I'm glad she is our Governor!

***

See the photo of Sarah Palin and Dawson Dolly on page 101

An Alaskan resident for 24 years, Cindy Godbey has spent 17 of those years entertaining as "Dawson Dolly", a reformed madam who found the Lord and set out to spread His love. Cindy herself found the Lord in 1997. Since then she has brought joy and laughter to all she meets. With her genuine love of Alaska and her compassionate nature, Cindy has expanded her repertoire to include inspirational speaking and entertaining for private parties and conferences. She has traveled from the Top of the World to Texas and everywhere in between for speaking engagements, and has visited many churches to share her testimony. While Cindy's ambition is simply "to touch people's hearts", she has boundless charisma and inner joy that adds dazzle and a personal touch to any gathering.

If you would like to book Cindy for an appearance at your function, please contact her at **dawsondollys@yahoo.com.**

Credits
Dolly's wonderful array of costumes are made by Jean Worley of Skagway. Jean and Cindy collaborate on the costume designs. Cindy loves fabric shopping for "Dolly" in New York City!
Cindy's stories have been edited by Heather Mjolsness of Whitehorse, Yukon.
Cover design is by Cindy's niece, Cara Sanderson Bown, of Cleveland, Ohio. She is a graphic artist and designer.
Layout of this book was done by Lorna McLellan of Atlin, BC.
Thanks to Marian Holler, Magic Mud Studio in Atlin, BC for fine tuning the final layout.
Front cover photography by Andrew Cremata.
Back cover photography by Heather Mjolsness.

Beautiful Atlin Lake
Photo by Lorna McLellan

With this Ring...
Photo by Gary Haeger

Julie Wilson at Crosswinds Lake
Photo by Kirk Wilson

Dawson Dolly, Daniel Johnson &
his daughter Danyka, with his eagles

MORE PHOTO MEMORIES

Sarah Palin and Dawson Dolly at the lovely
Jewell Gardens of Skagway, Alaska
Photo by Scott Logan

Dawson Dolly receiving "Tour Guide of the Year"
from Princess Cruise Lines

DOLLY'S ADVENTURES AT THE TOP OF THE WORLD

Land of the Midnight Sun
Photo by Cindy Shults

Welcome to Barrow! Photo by Cindy Shults

Barrow, Alaska Walrus
Photo by Cindy Shults

A FUN DAY WITH DOLLY

Dolly & her Nugget Band
Photo by Stacy Eaton

Dolly & the Band
Steam Engine #73
White Pass & Yukon Route RR
Photo by Stacy Eaton

White Pass & Yukon Route RR
Gary Danielson & Michael Brandt
Photo by Stacy Eaton

Dolly gets a helping hand
Photo by Stacy Eaton

Julian "Mr. Smile"
Future NCL Shore Excursion Manager
Photo by Alina Juliachs

Smile - God Loves You!